The Divorce Instinct

Rebuilding a Financial Identity After the Split That Took Half of Everything

Jordan Ellis

First edition, 2026

Published by Jordan Ellis

This book is intended for general educational and reflective purposes only. It is not a substitute for professional financial, legal, medical, or mental health advice, diagnosis, or treatment. Always seek the advice of a qualified professional with any questions regarding your specific circumstances. Never disregard professional advice or delay seeking it because of something you have read in this book. Names and identifying details in any illustrative examples are anonymous/archetypal composites, not depictions of a single real individual.

Contents

Foreword

I've now written enough of these books to notice a pattern in what readers write back to tell me. The ones about spending, saving, earning — those letters describe a behavior someone wants to change. This book is different. The letters that led me here didn't describe a behavior. They described a person who used to exist and didn't anymore: the half of a couple who checked a joint balance without thinking, who split a grocery bill without doing math, who had, for years, an entire financial self that only worked because someone else's name was on the account too. Divorce didn't just end a marriage for these readers. It repossessed an identity they'd built for a decade or two and never once had to build alone.

That's the book I kept getting asked to write, sideways, in letters that were technically about something else — a woman who couldn't bring herself to close a joint account eighteen months after the papers were signed, a man who'd started hoarding cash in a way that frightened him, a reader who admitted, almost as a joke, that she still calculated her net worth the way she and her ex-husband used to calculate it together, as though he were still a silent co-signer on a decision he'd stopped being part of years ago.

I want to be honest about the limits of what's ahead. This is not a book about the legal mechanics of divorce, and it has no opinion about your specific settlement, your custody arrangement, or whether the split was fair. Other books, and better-qualified professionals, handle that terrain. This book is about something narrower and, I've come to think, more neglected: what happens inside a person's financial nervous system when a shared identity gets cut in half, and why the reconstruction that follows is so much harder, and so much stranger, than anyone warns you it will be.

If you're reading this mid-divorce, newly divorced, or years out and still finding old reflexes in your hands, this book was written for exactly where you are.

— Jordan Ellis

Introduction

There is a specific moment, months after the papers are final, that catches almost everyone off guard, and it rarely looks like grief from the outside. You're standing in a grocery store, or opening a banking app, or signing a lease with only your own name on the line, and you reach for a decision-making process that isn't there anymore — a half-second pause where you used to check in, mentally, with a person who is no longer checking in with you. The dishwasher breaks and some part of you still runs the old subroutine: *we'll figure out how to split this.* Except there's no we. There's just you, standing in a kitchen that's either newly yours or still legally half someone else's, holding a decision that used to be shared and now, for the first time in years, is entirely and only your own.

This book is about that moment, and about the long, uneven stretch of time on either side of it — the financial identity that gets built inside a long relationship, the specific way it gets torn apart when the relationship ends, and the work, often clumsy and rarely linear, of building a new one that belongs to you alone. It is not a book about who gets the house, or how to split a retirement account, or what a fair settlement looks like on paper. Plenty of professionals are better equipped to help with those questions than a book like this one, and this book has no opinion on your specific numbers. What it has instead is a close look at something almost nobody prepares you for: the psychological work of unwinding a merged financial self back into an individual one, and the specific, predictable ways that unwinding goes wrong.

Here is the master thesis this whole book stands on, the sentence you should be able to repeat to a friend with no footnote attached: divorce doesn't just split a couple's money in half — it dissolves the financial self you built as one half of a pair, and what comes next isn't recovery of the person you used to be. It's construction of someone new, built for the first time, alone. That distinction matters more than it sounds like it should. Recovery implies a known destination — get back to how things were, restore the old equilibrium, heal the wound until the scar is the only sign anything happened. Construction implies something harder and, ultimately, more honest: there is no old financial self to return to, because that self was never really yours in the first place. It was a joint structure, built by two people, and it can't be handed back to you intact just because one of the builders left.

It's worth being precise, early, about why this particular loss is so hard to name, let alone grieve properly. When a marriage ends, everyone around you understands, more or less, that you're grieving the relationship — the partner, the shared history, the future you'd planned that isn't happening now. Friends show up for that grief. They bring food for that grief. What almost nobody shows up for, because almost nobody names it as a real and separate loss, is the disappearance of an entire financial identity: the joint checking account you never had to think about, the shared sense of "our money" that quietly organized a thousand small decisions a year, the specific competence of being one half of a functioning financial team rather than the whole of a financial team by yourself. That identity took years to build. It dissolves in the time it takes a court to finalize paperwork, and almost nobody sends flowers for it.

Consider what "our money" actually was, before it stopped being a workable phrase. It wasn't just a joint account, though it was probably that too. It was a whole invisible operating system — who worried about which bills, who made the big calls and who deferred, whose salary quietly subsidized whose ambitions, whose spending habits the other person had learned to plan around without ever discussing it directly. You didn't build that system consciously, the way you might build a budget. It accreted, year over year, the way any long-term system between two people accretes — through a thousand small negotiations so routine you stopped noticing them as negotiations at all. And then, in the space of a legal process that often moves faster than the emotional one underneath it, that entire operating system got shut off, and you were handed back a version of yourself that had to run everything alone, on a system that had never once been tested for solo operation, because it was never built to run that way.

This is the part worth flagging plainly, because it changes how you'll read everything ahead: the difficulty you're having isn't a sign that you're bad with money, or emotionally fragile, or somehow worse at this than people who seem to "bounce back" faster. What you're experiencing has a real mechanism behind it, studied by real researchers, and it has almost nothing to do with financial literacy. You can know exactly how to build a budget, read a credit report, and calculate compound interest, and still find yourself standing in a kitchen unable to make a two-hundred-dollar decision that used to take you thirty seconds, because the difficulty was never about the math. It's about the fact that the *self* who used to make that decision, calmly, automatically, as half of a pair, doesn't exist in the same form anymore, and the self who's replacing her hasn't finished being built yet.

It also helps to say why this book uses the word "instinct" at all, since a reader encountering this volume as part of a longer library might reasonably wonder how a psychological rupture this specific and this circumstantial belongs alongside patterns that show up in every financial life, married or not, divorced or not. The answer is that divorce doesn't create a new mechanism out of nothing. It activates several very old ones — attachment, identity fusion, loss aversion, social comparison — that were already sitting quietly underneath ordinary financial behavior, and forces them into unusually sharp relief, all at once, under real pressure. The instincts this book describes aren't unique to divorce. Divorce is simply the event that makes them impossible to miss, which is exactly why studying this rupture closely teaches you something true about financial psychology more broadly, not only about this one life event.

It helps to say clearly, before going further, what this book assumes and what it doesn't. This book assumes you are the one navigating the aftermath — regardless of who initiated the divorce, regardless of whether it was amicable or bitter, regardless of whether you're the higher earner or the lower one, the one who kept the house or the one who moved out. The mechanisms in these pages show up across all of those variations, because they aren't about the specifics of your split. They're about what happens, psychologically, when a merged financial identity gets separated, and that process has recognizable shapes no matter which side of the settlement you sat on. This book also assumes something that deserves saying honestly, up front: the difficulty described here is not exclusive to divorce, even though divorce is this book's primary and central subject. A handful of chapters ahead will gesture, briefly, at the same underlying mechanism showing up after other kinds of relationship-ending loss — the end of a long-term partnership that never involved a legal marriage, or the death of a spouse, which produces its own version of a shared financial identity suddenly, unwillingly, becoming an individual one again. Those gestures are brief and secondary. This is a book about divorce, written primarily and specifically for people navigating divorce. But the mechanism itself, once you can see it clearly, turns out to be a little more universal than the specific life event that triggers it, and naming that honestly seemed more useful than pretending divorce is the only door this particular room has.

There's a reason this specific gap in the literature exists, and it's worth understanding before the chapters begin. Most books about divorce and money focus, understandably, on the settlement itself — how assets get divided, what a fair split looks like, how to protect yourself legally and financially during the process. That's real, important work, and this book isn't trying to replace it. But that work almost universally treats the settlement as the finish line, the same mistaken assumption another book in this library makes about disclosure inside a still-intact marriage: get the paperwork right, and the rest more or less follows. It doesn't. The settlement divides the assets. It does nothing to divide, or rebuild, the psychological architecture that spent years organizing itself around a partnership that no longer exists. You can walk away from a mediation table with an entirely fair, entirely reasonable settlement and still spend the next three years making financial decisions that make no sense on paper, because the paper was never where the actual problem lived.

Consider, for a moment, three of the specific ways this reconstruction tends to go wrong, because you'll recognize a version of at least one of them, and naming them early gives you a map for the chapters ahead. Some people, in the aftermath, over-correct hard in the direction of control — building a financial life so rigid, so defended, so allergic to any form of shared decision-making or even ordinary risk, that safety curdles into its own kind of prison, a fortress built so thoroughly that nothing, including good things, can get back in. Others do close to the opposite: they stay financially entangled with an ex-partner far longer than logistics actually require, not out of confusion about the settlement terms but out of a guilt, or a grief, or a fear of the finality that full separation represents — still covering a bill that isn't theirs anymore, still checking a shared account that was supposed to close a year ago, still, in some quiet way, keeping one hand on a life that has already legally ended. And a third group finds themselves sabotaging the fresh start directly in front of them — refusing to open a new account in their own name only, refusing to update a beneficiary, refusing to build anything that feels genuinely, unambiguously theirs — because building something new can feel, in the moment, like agreeing that the old life is really over, and some part of the self isn't ready to sign that agreement yet, even after the legal one is long since signed.

None of these three patterns, and none of the others the chapters ahead will name, are failures of character or intelligence. They're what happens, predictably, when a financial identity that was built for two people suddenly has to run on one operating system, without a manual, usually while its owner is also managing genuine grief, genuine anger, genuine logistics, and often genuine fear about the future, all at the same time. The reconstruction work this book is about doesn't happen in a vacuum of calm reflection. It happens while you're also doing everything else divorce requires, which is exactly why it goes wrong as often as it does, and exactly why almost nobody manages to do it cleanly on the first attempt.

Here's what the chapters ahead do, and why they're built the way they are. Each one opens with a close, specific scene — a person, a moment, a financial decision that reveals the pattern in motion — built for psychological clarity rather than drawn from any single real account, because the shape of the pattern matters here, not the specifics of any one life. Each chapter then names the actual mechanism underneath the scene, grounded in real, verifiable research — never a manufactured statistic dressed up to sound authoritative, never a study invented to make a point land harder than the honest evidence supports. Each chapter counts what the pattern actually costs, not just financially but in the quieter currency of confidence, trust in your own judgment, and the pace of your own healing. And each chapter closes with concrete overrides — psychological moves, not products, platforms, or account types, because the goal here was never to tell you which bank to use. It was to change how you relate to the decision itself.

One thing worth saying honestly before the first chapter begins: this book will not make the reconstruction painless, and it won't make it fast. Anyone who tells you a formerly-married financial identity rebuilds itself cleanly within some tidy window — six months, a year, "once the dust settles" — is selling you a timeline the actual research doesn't support. What this book can offer instead is something narrower and, in practice, more useful: a map of the specific ways this rebuilding tends to go sideways, named clearly enough that you can recognize your own version of it while it's happening, rather than only in hindsight, months or years after a pattern has already cost you something real.

You should expect, reading these chapters, to see yourself in more than one of them, sometimes in contradictory ways within the same week — rigid about one account and recklessly entangled about another, sabotaging your own fresh start in one domain while white-knuckling total control in a different one. That's not a flaw in how this book is organized. It's how the actual rebuilding tends to work: unevenly, in fits and starts, one domain of a financial life often years ahead of another. Read for whichever chapter lands closest to where you actually are right now, and don't be surprised if that changes as your own reconstruction moves forward.

It also matters how differently this reconstruction lands depending on where a person sits in their own life when the divorce arrives. A person divorcing at twenty-eight, before children, before a mortgage, before two decades of compounding joint decisions, faces a real version of everything this book describes, but a lighter one — fewer accounts entangled, fewer years of habit to untangle, more runway left to build the new self this book keeps describing. A person divorcing at fifty-eight, after three decades of marriage, after raising children now grown, after building an entire adult identity as half of a specific pair, faces the same mechanisms in a considerably heavier form, often with less time and less energy to do the rebuilding than a younger reader might have.

This book doesn't assume a single age or a single life stage. The scenes ahead skew, for narrative variety, across a range of ages and circumstances deliberately, because the mechanisms themselves don't confine themselves to any one decade of life. A reader in her late twenties and a reader in his early sixties will likely each recognize themselves in different scenes, for different reasons, and both readings are exactly what this book was built for.

It's also worth saying honestly, before the chapters begin, that money is rarely the only casualty of a divorce, and this book doesn't pretend financial reconstruction happens in isolation from everything else a divorce disrupts — friendships that quietly take sides, a sense of home that has to be rebuilt somewhere new, a parenting relationship that has to be renegotiated from scratch, a private identity outside the marriage that may not have been exercised in years. This book focuses narrowly on the financial dimension of that larger reconstruction, not because the financial dimension is the most important one, but because it's the one almost nobody else is writing about directly, and because money, as this whole library keeps arguing, has a way of making psychological patterns visible that might otherwise stay abstract. If you're doing other kinds of rebuilding alongside the work in these pages — with a therapist, with friends, with time itself — that work matters at least as much as anything in this book, and nothing here is meant to replace it.

Let's start with the ledger itself — the specific, disorienting moment when "ours" becomes "yours," and what that word actually asks of you that nobody warns you about in advance.

Chapter 1 — The Ledger That Used to Say "Ours"

For eleven years, she never once looked at a bank balance and thought the word *mine*. It was always *ours* — the joint checking account they'd opened three weeks into the marriage, back when opening it had felt like the most obvious, most romantic administrative task either of them had ever done together. She could have told you the balance within a hundred dollars on any given day without checking, not because she tracked it obsessively, but because it lived in her the way a home address lives in you: absorbed, automatic, never requiring conscious retrieval. The account had a name they'd half-joked about — "the house fund," even after the house was bought, because the name had stuck the way old jokes do inside a marriage. It held their vacations, their emergency cushion, the slow accumulation of two incomes braided into a single, shared financial life neither of them had to think about as an achievement, because it had simply always been the water they swam in.

The morning she opened her first solo account, eight months after the papers were signed, she sat in the bank parking lot afterward for eleven minutes without starting the car. Nothing had gone wrong. The banker had been kind, efficient, entirely unremarkable in the way a routine transaction should be. And still, she sat there, staring at a debit card with only her own name embossed on it, feeling something she couldn't immediately place — not sadness exactly, not relief exactly, something closer to vertigo, the specific disorientation of holding proof that a version of yourself now existed that had never existed before. She had been a financial half of something for eleven years. This card was evidence that she was now, for the first time since her mid-twenties, a whole.

The vertigo didn't fade the way she expected it to. Small decisions that should have taken seconds started taking minutes. Standing in a hardware store choosing between two paint colors, she found herself reaching, reflexively, for a consultation that no longer existed — not a memory of a specific conversation, just the ghost of the process itself, the half-formed sense that a decision like this used to get run past someone else first, even when it hadn't, technically, required his opinion at all. She'd choose a color eventually, alone, and it would be fine. But the choosing itself had changed shape, and she couldn't tell, in the moment, whether what she was mourning was him specifically, or the entire decision-making apparatus that had quietly assumed his presence for over a decade.

A different version of this same rupture showed up for a man two states away, four years into his own divorce, in a domain that had nothing to do with daily spending at all. He and his ex-wife had built a joint investment strategy over sixteen years of marriage — nothing exotic, a fairly standard mix of retirement accounts and a modest taxable brokerage account they'd funded together, decided on together, checked together every few months over a glass of wine on a Sunday evening that had become, without either of them planning it, a small ritual. After the divorce, his share of that portfolio moved into accounts with only his name on them, exactly as the settlement specified, exactly as it should have. And for almost two years afterward, he found he genuinely couldn't look at the statements. Not out of confusion about the numbers — he understood the numbers perfectly well, better than most people his age. He avoided them because the portfolio itself had been, for sixteen years, a joint project, a thing they'd built together the way some couples build a garden, and looking at it alone felt less like checking an investment and more like visiting a grave. The money hadn't changed. What it represented had.

A third version of this pattern shows up further from the marriage bed than either of these two scenes, in a domain this book's mitigation clause promised to address honestly: the end of a long-term partnership that never involved a legal marriage at all. A woman in her late thirties, together with her partner for nine years, unmarried by mutual choice but financially intertwined in nearly every practical way — a shared lease, a shared car loan, a joint account they'd built with the same casual permanence as any married couple's — found, when the relationship ended, that she had almost none of the legal scaffolding divorced couples take for granted. No settlement, no mediator, no court date forcing the financial unwinding into a defined process with a defined endpoint. Just two adults, deeply entangled financially after nine years, trying to informally negotiate an untangling with no formal structure to lean on at all. The psychological rupture she experienced — the vertigo, the reflexive reaching for a decision-making partner who no longer existed — was, by her own account, indistinguishable from what her recently divorced sister had described going through the year before. The legal instrument was different. The financial identity being dissolved was not.

A fourth version of this same rupture shows up in a domain most people don't think to name as financial at all: credit history. A man in his early fifties, divorced after twenty-two years, discovered the rupture not in a bank parking lot but in a mortgage broker's office, applying for a loan on a smaller condo, when the broker pulled a credit report built almost entirely around a joint history he no longer had access to explain. The score was still respectable. But every account on the report told the story of a marriage — a joint card opened the year they married, a joint auto loan from a car they'd sold years before the divorce, a length-of-credit-history calculation quietly built on accounts he could no longer point to as evidence of his own standalone reliability. He hadn't lost the score. He'd lost the narrative the score used to tell about him as an individual, and rebuilding a credit identity that told his story alone, rather than the couple's story, took the better part of two years of patient, deliberate account-building he'd never once had to think about during the marriage, because during the marriage, he'd never needed a story that was only his.

What all three of these people shared, underneath the specifics, was the same disorienting discovery: the financial self they'd been operating as for years wasn't a personality trait they could simply carry forward alone. It was a joint structure, co-authored, and no amount of individual competence could substitute for the fact that half its architecture had just walked out the door.

What's actually happening

The clearest lens for understanding this rupture comes from the self-expansion model developed by psychologists Arthur Aron and Elaine Aron, whose decades of research into close relationships produced one of the most consistently replicated findings in relationship science: as a relationship deepens, partners don't simply grow closer while remaining psychologically separate. They begin to include the other person, cognitively, as part of the self — a process the Arons and their collaborators have documented through measures of how people literally confuse their own traits and resources with their partner's traits and resources when asked to recall them quickly. A long-married person asked to list "my resources" will often, measurably, include things that are technically their spouse's — a skill, a habit, a financial cushion — because at a cognitive level, the boundary between self and partner has genuinely blurred. This isn't sentimentality. It's a documented feature of how the mind represents a close relationship, and it applies with particular force to money, because money is one of the most concretely shared resources most couples ever build together.

This matters enormously for understanding what happens during divorce, because it means the joint account wasn't simply a convenient shared tool sitting outside either partner's individual identity. It was, in a real cognitive sense, partially inside each partner's identity — a resource the self-expansion research would predict gets processed, at some level, as *mine* and *theirs* simultaneously, rather than cleanly as *ours* in the tidy, external sense the word usually implies. When that account closes, or splits, or gets divided by a court order, the self-expansion research offers a genuinely useful reframe for why it feels less like losing a possession and more like losing a piece of self: because, cognitively, that's close to what's actually happening. You are not simply losing access to funds. You are losing a portion of a self that had, over years, expanded to include another person's resources as though they were partly your own — and now has to contract, abruptly, back down to a boundary it hasn't occupied in a long time, if it ever occupied it as an adult at all.

The Arons developed a simple, widely used measurement tool alongside this research, worth pointing out because it makes the abstract idea concrete: the Inclusion of Other in the Self scale, a set of overlapping circles a person selects between to represent how much they experience their own identity as overlapping with a partner's, ranging from circles that barely touch to circles nearly superimposed on one another.

Long-married couples reliably select the most overlapping options on that scale, and the credit-history scenario above illustrates precisely what a court-ordered separation of finances asks of someone sitting at that end of the spectrum: not simply dividing an asset, but forcibly pulling apart two circles that had, by any honest measurement, become nearly one. The mortgage broker wasn't asking the man to explain a stranger's financial history. He was asking him to draw a boundary around a self that hadn't had a distinct boundary, in that particular sense, in over two decades.

There's a second, related piece here, because it explains why this contraction feels so much harder for people who married young or married for a very long time. The self-expansion research suggests the degree of cognitive overlap between partners tends to deepen the longer and more thoroughly two people's lives interweave — which means the eleven-year marriage and the sixteen-year investment partnership described above weren't simply "long relationships" in some generic sense. They represented over a decade of continuous, compounding cognitive merger, the financial self quietly expanding, year after year, to include another person's habits, resources, and decision-making style as though they were simply part of how this particular person now operated. Unwinding that isn't like returning a borrowed object. It's closer to relearning where your own hand ends and someone else's used to begin — a boundary that genuinely has to be rebuilt, not simply remembered, because for the length of the marriage, that boundary functionally didn't exist in the same place it does now.

This reframe also explains a specific detail from the man's portfolio-avoidance story: why looking at the numbers alone felt, to him, less like reviewing an investment and more like visiting a grave. Grief research, most notably the work of psychologist George Bonanno and his decades of study into how people actually process loss, has documented that grief doesn't attach only to people who die. It attaches to anything that represented a significant, ongoing investment of identity and meaning, and a financial structure two people built together over sixteen years — Sunday evenings, shared decisions, a small accumulating record of a life chosen jointly — qualifies as exactly that kind of investment, even though nobody died and the relationship simply, legally, ended. Bonanno's broader research is also worth pausing on for what it gets right about resilience: most people, across most kinds of loss including divorce, do eventually adapt, often faster and more completely than either they or the people around them initially expect. That's a genuinely hopeful finding, and it's worth holding alongside the harder truth that the adaptation isn't instant, and that the specific object triggering the grief — in this case, an investment portfolio — deserves to be recognized as a real site of loss rather than dismissed as "just money," a dismissal that tends to make people feel strange or excessive for grieving something a court finalized cleanly on paper.

There's an important distinction worth drawing here, one this whole book returns to in different forms: the difference between financial grief that's proportionate to a real loss, and financial grief that's calcified into avoidance. It's entirely reasonable, and healthy, to feel the vertigo described above the first time you open a solo account, or the first time you look at a portfolio that used to be shared. What turns that reasonable grief into a genuine cost — the subject of the next section — is when the avoidance becomes the standing strategy, month after month, rather than a passing wave that eventually recedes as the new financial self gets built out enough to stand on its own.

Kenneth Doka's research on what he termed disenfranchised grief adds a final, necessary layer to this mechanism, and it's worth sitting with because it explains why almost nobody prepares you for any of this in advance. Doka's work describes grief that isn't socially recognized or validated as legitimate grief — losses society doesn't extend the normal rituals of mourning to, because the loss doesn't fit the culturally expected shape of a "real" loss. Divorce grief broadly fits this category; almost nobody brings a casserole when a marriage ends the way they would if a spouse had died. But the specific grief of losing a joint financial identity sits even further out on that margin, disenfranchised twice over — first because it's divorce-related grief, and second because it's grief over something as seemingly unsentimental as a bank account, which culture doesn't code as an appropriate thing to mourn at all. Nobody sends flowers for a closed joint account. That absence of recognition doesn't make the loss smaller. It just makes it lonelier, and considerably harder to name, which is a large part of why this book exists.

What it costs you

The immediate cost is the one both people in the opening scenes experienced directly: a specific, disorienting paralysis around decisions that used to be automatic, showing up at exactly the moment in life when a person most needs to be making clear, confident financial choices. New leases, new insurance policies, new retirement contribution elections, new emergency funds built from scratch — all of it has to happen during precisely the period when the decision-making self is least equipped to move quickly, because the self doing the deciding is, in a real sense, still under construction. This isn't a minor inconvenience. Decisions delayed during this window — an insurance policy left unupdated, a beneficiary form left unchanged, an emergency fund left unbuilt — compound in ways that can genuinely hurt someone's financial position for years after the divorce itself is long settled.

There's a subtler cost that shows up as a kind of chronic under-confidence in one's own financial judgment, even in people who were, by any external measure, entirely capable before the marriage and remain entirely capable now. Because the joint decision-making apparatus ran for so long, and ran well enough that neither partner had much reason to test their solo judgment against it, divorce forces a kind of judgment audit nobody asked for — an abrupt discovery of exactly how much of one's financial confidence was actually borrowed, or co-produced, rather than independently held. That discovery, arriving all at once, in the middle of an already difficult period, can produce a level of self-doubt wildly disproportionate to a person's actual competence, because the competence was always real. It just hadn't been exercised solo in a very long time, and the gap between "I've never had to do this alone" and "I can't do this" gets collapsed, unfairly, far too often.

There's a cost, too, to relationships beyond the marriage itself — specifically, to the people around a divorced person who don't understand why a seemingly simple financial task is taking so long, or triggering so much visible distress. A friend or family member watching someone struggle to open a solo account, or avoid a portfolio statement for two years, can easily misread the struggle as financial incompetence, or excessive attachment to an ex, or simply "not being over it yet" in some judgmental sense — none of which captures what's actually happening. That misreading, however well-intentioned, adds a layer of social cost on top of an already disorienting private one: not just the vertigo itself, but the isolation of having the vertigo misunderstood by people who mean well and simply don't have the framework to see what's actually going on.

Left unaddressed for long enough, this rupture has a way of quietly narrowing a person's financial life rather than simply delaying its rebuild. Someone who never fully processes the loss of the joint financial self can end up permanently under-building the solo one — carrying a persistent, low-grade sense that any financial structure they build alone is somehow provisional, less real, less legitimate than what existed before, even years after the divorce. That underlying sense of provisionality tends to produce exactly the kind of hesitation the chapters ahead will keep naming in different forms: the account never quite optimized, the investment never quite made, the insurance never quite updated, not because the knowledge is missing but because some part of the self is still waiting, quietly, for a version of "ours" to come back and finish the job.

There's a final cost worth spelling out honestly, because it's the one most likely to blindside a reader who feels, on the surface, like they've moved past this chapter's territory already: the ledger rupture doesn't announce itself only once, at the moment of the split. It tends to recur — at tax season, when a joint filing status disappears for the first time in years; at a child's wedding, when the old habit of splitting a cost with an ex-spouse resurfaces briefly and painfully; at a class reunion, when someone asks, innocently, "how's married life treating you," and the financial identity that used to answer that question with an easy, automatic *we* has to reroute, again, into a solitary *I*. Each recurrence is smaller than the original rupture, usually. But each one is real, and expecting the grief to be finished after the first hard year is one of the more common, and more unnecessary, sources of frustration people carry into this specific kind of rebuilding.

There's a practical cost, too, in domains that don't announce themselves as emotional at all, illustrated directly by the credit-history scenario. A rebuilt credit identity, a rebuilt insurance history, a rebuilt record of on-time payments under a single name — all of it takes real time to accumulate, and lenders, insurers, and underwriters have no mechanism for crediting a person with the two decades of joint financial reliability that came before. The instruments that measure financial trustworthiness were never built to recognize a self mid-reconstruction. They only measure the self that already exists on paper, which means a genuinely reliable, financially sound person can look, on a report, meaningfully less established than they actually are, simply because the measurement resets at the exact moment a person can least afford for it to.

The overrides

Name the loss as a real loss, out loud, to yourself first. Before anything practical changes, it helps to say plainly, even privately: *I am not just dividing assets. I am losing a version of myself that only existed as half of a partnership, and that loss deserves to be treated as real.* This isn't self-indulgence. It's an accurate diagnosis, and an accurate diagnosis is the only thing that will let you stop mistaking ordinary grief for a personal failure to "get it together" financially.

The Move: build one new solo financial ritual within the first sixty days, on purpose, before you feel ready. Not a major decision — something small and symbolic, like reviewing your own solo budget every Sunday evening at the same time the old joint check-in used to happen, or opening your first fully independent account even if you don't need it immediately for anything practical. The goal isn't efficiency. It's giving your nervous system a new, repeated, embodied experience of solo competence to start overwriting the old joint one, because waiting to feel ready before building anything new usually means waiting indefinitely — readiness tends to follow the repetition, not precede it.

Give the avoided task a deadline shorter than your instinct wants. If there's a specific account, statement, or portfolio you've been avoiding the way the man in this chapter avoided his — pick a date within the next two weeks, not "eventually," and tell one other person that date out loud, so there's a small amount of accountability attached to it. The avoidance isn't laziness. It's a genuine grief response, and grief responses, left entirely to their own timeline, will often extend far longer than they need to. A firm, near-term deadline doesn't erase the discomfort of finally looking. It just makes sure the looking happens before the avoidance calcifies into the kind of permanent under-building described above.

Separate "this feels wrong" from "this is wrong." When a new solo financial decision produces that specific vertigo — the reflexive reach for a consultation partner who isn't there — pause and ask directly: is this decision actually risky, or does it simply feel unfamiliar because I've never made this exact kind of choice alone before? Most of the time, the discomfort is unfamiliarity wearing the costume of danger. Naming that difference explicitly, in the moment, is often enough to let the decision get made rather than endlessly deferred.

Let the grief be specific rather than generic. If you notice a wave of sadness or disorientation attached to a particular financial object — a portfolio, an account, a specific recurring bill you used to split — resist the instinct to immediately generalize it into "I'm still not over the divorce." Ask instead, precisely: what am I actually mourning about this specific thing? Sometimes the honest answer is smaller and more manageable than the sweeping one — you're not mourning the marriage in that moment, you're mourning a Sunday-evening ritual, or a sixteen-year project, or a specific competence you used to take for granted. Specific grief resolves faster than generic grief, because you can actually finish grieving something you've named precisely.

Expect recurrence, and don't let it convince you that you've regressed. When the rupture resurfaces at tax season, or a reunion, or an unexpected reminder, treat it as a known, ordinary feature of this particular kind of loss rather than evidence that the earlier work didn't take. A grief that recurs in smaller waves over years isn't a grief that failed to resolve. It's simply how this kind of loss, disenfranchised and largely unnamed by the people around you, tends to actually move through a person over time.

Hold a small, deliberate closing ritual for the accounts that are actually ending. When a joint account finally closes, or a joint card finally gets cancelled, mark it as something rather than letting it pass as pure paperwork — a note in a journal, a conversation with a friend, even just a moment of conscious acknowledgment that a real structure, built over real years, has just ended. Cultures without an established ritual for this kind of loss tend to leave people processing it in fragments, over months, without ever fully registering that it happened. A small, self-authored ritual gives the mind something more concrete to file the ending under than a bank's automated closure notice ever will.

Rebuild the credit story deliberately, rather than letting it rebuild itself by accident. If your credit history, like the man's in this chapter, reads as a joint narrative rather than an individual one, take one deliberate step toward giving it its own standalone story — a small, solely held account, a bill reported in your name only, a modest line of credit built and maintained on your own. This isn't about the score alone. It's about giving the institutions that measure financial trustworthiness a true, current record of the individual person actually standing in front of them now.

Tell one person the specific shape of your own version of this rupture. Because the grief this chapter describes is disenfranchised, it rarely gets acknowledged unless you actively name it to someone else first. Choose one trusted person and describe, plainly, which specific object, account, or moment has carried the most weight for you — not the whole divorce, just this one piece of it. Being witnessed in a loss that culture doesn't automatically recognize tends to make it considerably easier to carry.

The Rule to Remember: you are not trying to become who you were before you were half of a couple — you are building someone new, for the first time, and the unfamiliarity you feel is the sound of real construction, not evidence that something's broken.

Chapter 2 — The Guilt You Keep Paying Down

Fourteen months after the divorce was final, he was still paying his ex-wife's car insurance. Not because the settlement required it — it didn't, and both attorneys had confirmed as much in writing. He kept paying it because every time he sat down to cancel the automatic transfer, some quiet, insistent voice in his chest told him it would be cruel to stop, that she'd struggled to find steady work since the split, that a man who could afford it and chose not to help was, on some level, not a good person. He never mentioned it to anyone. It felt, privately, like the last decent thing he could do for someone he'd once promised to take care of, even though the promise itself no longer legally or practically applied.

What made the pattern strange, if he'd stopped to examine it honestly, was that he wasn't actually helping out of ongoing tenderness toward her. Their conversations had grown cold and businesslike, confined mostly to logistics about their two children. He didn't particularly want to talk to her. He wasn't hoping for reconciliation. If anything, the calls that did happen left him drained and a little resentful. And yet the automatic transfer kept firing every month, a hundred and ninety dollars he no longer owed, moving out of his account into hers, propelled by something that had almost nothing to do with how he actually felt about her anymore and almost everything to do with how he felt about himself if he stopped.

A different version of the same guilt showed up for a woman two years into her own divorce, in a completely different financial shape. She and her ex-husband had agreed, amicably enough, to sell the house and split the proceeds — a clean, sensible plan neither of them disputed. But eighteen months after the sale closed, she still hadn't touched her half of the money. It sat in a savings account earning almost nothing, untouched, while she continued renting a smaller apartment she could genuinely no longer afford long-term without dipping into savings she'd built independently, before the marriage. When a friend finally asked her, gently, why she hadn't used any of the house money to ease her own situation, she didn't have a clean answer. The honest one, when she finally found it, surprised her: some part of her felt that spending "his" half of the house —

even though it was legally, entirely, unambiguously her own now — would be taking something from him that she hadn't fully earned the right to take. The money wasn't his anymore. Nobody disputed that on paper. But some part of her hadn't finished the negotiation the paper had already settled.

A third version of this pattern surfaces in a domain further from the direct financial mechanics of the split: a man whose wife died after a long illness, rather than a divorce, found himself, three years later, still maintaining her small monthly donation to a charity she'd supported for over a decade — a donation that had, admittedly, meant something to her, but that he continued not out of genuine ongoing commitment to the cause, and not because he'd ever discussed continuing it with anyone, but because stopping it felt, in some inarticulate way, like a second death, a final severing he wasn't ready to authorize. The mechanism here is close to identical to the two divorce scenes above, even though the triggering loss was entirely different: a financial action, continued past its practical necessity, functioning as a way to avoid the full, final weight of a separation the rest of the person's life has already, technically, absorbed.

A fourth version of this pattern shows up in a quieter, less visible register: a woman two years divorced who had stopped any direct payments to her ex-husband entirely, exactly as the settlement specified, but who still, without quite admitting it to herself, kept a folder of receipts for every gift she'd bought their children that year, mentally tallying it against what she imagined he was spending, ready to produce the tally if he ever accused her of contributing less. There was no actual dispute happening. He'd never once suggested she wasn't pulling her weight. The folder existed purely to preempt a guilt she was certain would find her eventually, an accusation nobody had made, built and maintained against a version of the conflict that lived only in her own anticipation of it.

What's actually happening

It helps, before naming the mechanism directly, to notice what all four scenes in this chapter share structurally: in each one, the financial behavior in question had already stopped serving any practical function the person involved could clearly articulate, and yet continued anyway, propelled by something operating beneath conscious deliberation. This is worth calling out up front because it's easy to mistake this pattern, from the outside, for simple soft-heartedness or a failure to enforce a boundary. It's neither. It's a specific, well-documented psychological mechanism doing exactly what it evolved to do, and understanding the mechanism is the fastest route to actually changing the behavior it produces.

The clearest way to understand this pattern starts with a distinction well established in the loss-aversion research pioneered by psychologists Daniel Kahneman and Amos Tversky: people don't weigh gains and losses symmetrically. Losses register, psychologically, as considerably more painful than equivalent gains feel pleasurable — a finding that has shaped decades of behavioral economics research since. What's often left out of how that finding gets applied is that "loss" doesn't only mean financial loss. It can mean the loss of a relationship, an identity, a sense of moral standing in someone else's eyes, and a person navigating divorce is frequently trying to avoid several kinds of loss simultaneously, not just the practical kind. Continuing to pay an ex-spouse's insurance, or refusing to touch a legitimate share of settlement money, functions, underneath the surface, as a way of avoiding a loss that has nothing to do with the dollar amount involved: the loss of being the kind of person who provides, who is generous, who didn't simply walk away and stop caring the moment the paperwork cleared.

This connects directly to research on moral identity and self-concept maintenance, a body of work that has documented, across many contexts, how strongly people are motivated to act in ways consistent with a self-image they've built over years, even at real material cost to themselves. A person who has spent a decade or two of marriage occupying the identity of provider, protector, or caretaker doesn't shed that identity the moment a marriage legally ends. The identity persists, and behaviors that continue to express it — an unnecessary insurance payment, an untouched settlement, a maintained donation — aren't really about the ex-partner at all, however much they look that way from the outside. They're about the self, and the discomfort of becoming, abruptly, a different kind of person than the one you spent years understanding yourself to be.

There's a second layer worth sitting with, drawn from attachment research originating with John Bowlby and extended by decades of subsequent work, most notably by psychologist Mary Ainsworth. Attachment theory describes how deeply humans are wired to maintain proximity and connection to significant attachment figures, and how disrupting that bond — even a bond the conscious mind fully understands is over — triggers real, measurable distress that doesn't simply switch off because a legal process has concluded. A continued financial tie to an ex-spouse can function, whether or not the person maintaining it would ever describe it this way, as a form of continued proximity — a thread that keeps the attachment bond from having to be fully, finally severed all at once. This is part of why guilt is often the wrong word for what's actually driving the behavior, even though guilt is usually how it gets described. What's frequently underneath the guilt isn't really moral obligation. It's attachment, still functioning, still seeking a form of connection the conscious mind has already decided shouldn't exist anymore.

The third scenario — the widower maintaining his late wife's donation — makes this mechanism unusually visible, precisely because there's no residual romantic complication to muddy the picture. Nobody would accuse a grieving widower of secretly wanting his wife back in a way that implicates poor judgment; his continued donation reads clearly, to anyone who hears about it, as an act of love and loyalty rather than a confused entanglement. And yet the underlying mechanism — a financial action maintained past its practical necessity, functioning as a way to avoid a final severing — is structurally the same behavior the divorced man and woman are engaged in. This comparison matters, because it suggests the divorce versions of this pattern deserve the same compassionate reading, even though divorce, unlike death, tends to get read by everyone around it, including the person going through it, as something a person should simply be "over" by a specific, socially agreed-upon point. Attachment doesn't actually check which legal instrument ended the relationship before deciding how hard it is to sever. It responds to the depth and duration of the bond, and a fourteen-year marriage builds an attachment bond every bit as real as a spouse lost to illness, even though the culture around divorce rarely extends it the same patience.

There's a third piece here, specific to why this particular guilt is so persistent and so hard to argue yourself out of using logic alone. Research on rumination and moral emotion, including work associated with psychologist June Tangney's decades of study distinguishing guilt from shame, has found that guilt — as opposed to shame, which attacks the whole self — tends to be action-focused: guilt is triggered by a specific behavior a person believes was, or might be, wrong, and it resolves, psychologically, through a specific corrective action rather than through simple reassurance. This is part of why telling the guilty ex-spouse "you don't owe her anything anymore" so rarely lands, even when it's entirely, legally true. Guilt isn't actually asking for a verdict on whether the debt is owed. It's asking for an action that will let the guilt discharge itself — which is exactly what the continued insurance payment, or the untouched settlement, is quietly, ineffectively trying to provide. The problem isn't that the corrective action is wrong in principle. It's that this specific corrective action never actually resolves the guilt, because the guilt was never really about the insurance or the money in the first place.

The receipt-folder scenario adds one further piece: anticipatory guilt, a documented variant in which a person begins managing a feared future accusation before that accusation has ever actually been made, sometimes before there's any real evidence it ever will be. This is closely related to broader anxiety research on threat anticipation, which has found that the mind frequently treats a vividly imagined future criticism with nearly the same urgency as a real, present one, prompting real, effortful, present-tense behavior — keeping the folder, running the tally — in defense against something that exists only as a possibility. The folder wasn't protecting her from an actual dispute. It was protecting her from the discomfort of imagining one, which is a considerably harder thing to resolve through evidence, because no amount of real receipts will ever fully satisfy a fear that was never actually waiting on proof to begin with.

Taken together, these four scenarios point to a single, useful test worth carrying into any future moment this chapter's pattern shows up: ask whether the behavior in question is actually serving the other person, or whether it's serving a feeling inside yourself that has nothing to do with them at all. The man's insurance payment, the woman's untouched settlement, the receipt folder, all failed this test in the same way — each one presented itself as being about the ex-partner, and each one turned out, on close examination, to be almost entirely about the person doing the giving, the withholding, or the preemptive defending. That test doesn't make the underlying feeling go away. But it does make it considerably easier to see clearly, which is most of what the overrides below are built to help you do.

What it costs you

The most direct cost is financial, and it's worth stating plainly because it's often larger than people realize once they actually tally it: money continuing to flow toward an ex-partner past the point of genuine obligation is money not building the new, solo financial structure this whole book is about helping you construct. The hundred and ninety dollars a month is real money — over a year, well over two thousand dollars that could have gone toward an emergency fund the man in this chapter's opening scene didn't yet have, built during exactly the window when building one mattered most. The untouched settlement money is a similarly real cost, compounding in a low-yield account instead of paying down higher-interest debt, or funding a security deposit on a place the woman in the second scene could genuinely afford, or simply existing as the emergency cushion that would have let her sleep better at night during an already stressful year.

There's a subtler cost to the relationship with the ex-spouse itself, one that often surprises people once it's named. Continued, unnecessary financial entanglement doesn't typically produce the gratitude or goodwill the guilty party is unconsciously hoping it will. It more often produces confusion, or a low-grade sense on the other side that boundaries aren't being respected, or — in less generous cases — a quiet expectation that the payments will simply continue indefinitely, an expectation that becomes its own source of conflict once the paying partner eventually, inevitably, wants to stop. What was meant as generosity can curdle, over time, into a genuine source of friction precisely because it was never actually asked for, agreed to, or acknowledged as a real ongoing arrangement by either party.

There's a cost, too, to the process of severing the attachment bond itself — the actual psychological work this book keeps returning to, of rebuilding a financial identity that no longer includes the ex-spouse as a silent variable in every decision. Every month the unnecessary payment continues, the attachment bond gets a small, repeated reinforcement rather than the gradual weakening that time and distance would otherwise produce. This doesn't mean the person is choosing to stay attached on purpose. It means the mechanism maintaining the tie is working exactly as attachment mechanisms are designed to work, and it will keep working, quietly, for as long as the behavior that feeds it continues.

There's a specific cost that shows up around new relationships, worth naming honestly because it's rarely discussed. A person still financially entangled with an ex-spouse, even in small, seemingly generous ways, often struggles to fully explain the arrangement to a new partner, and the explanation, however well-intentioned, frequently lands badly — read as unresolved feelings, divided loyalty, or a boundary that hasn't been drawn where it needs to be. This isn't always an unfair read. Sometimes it's an accurate one, even when the person maintaining the payment would insist, honestly, that they've moved on. The behavior itself carries information that words alone can't fully override.

Finally, there's a cost to the guilt itself, left unresolved by an action that was never going to resolve it. Because the corrective behavior doesn't actually address the real source of the guilt — the abrupt, involuntary shift in identity from provider to individual — the guilt tends to persist alongside the payments rather than diminishing because of them. People in this pattern often report, years later, that they still feel a version of the same guilt even after finally stopping the unnecessary financial tie, because the guilt was never really a debt that money could settle. It was grief wearing a ledger entry, and ledger entries, however generous, were never going to be the thing that actually processed it.

There's a cost, finally, specific to the anticipatory version of this pattern illustrated by the receipt folder: the ongoing mental labor of tracking, tallying, and preparing a defense for an accusation that hasn't happened is real cognitive load, quietly draining attention and energy that could otherwise go toward the actual, present-tense work of parenting, earning, or rebuilding. A mind occupied with defending against an imagined future dispute has less available bandwidth for the real decisions in front of it, and this cost compounds precisely because it's invisible — nobody sees a folder of preemptive receipts and recognizes it as a tax on someone's daily attention, least of all the person quietly paying it.

The overrides

Separate the financial obligation from the moral feeling, in writing, once. Sit down and write out, plainly, exactly what you are legally and practically obligated to provide your ex-partner going forward, according to the actual settlement. Then, separately, write down what you feel obligated to provide, and notice the gap between the two lists. That gap is not evidence of an unresolved debt. It's a map of exactly where guilt has quietly expanded past the boundary the settlement already, deliberately, drew.

The Move: replace the ongoing payment with a single, defined, time-limited gesture instead. If some part of you genuinely wants to do one more generous thing before fully severing a financial tie — and that instinct isn't shameful, it can come from real decency — pick one specific, bounded action with a clear end: covering a single expense, one final time, with an explicit conversation that this is the last one. A defined gesture with a stated endpoint discharges the guilt far more effectively than an open-ended payment ever will, because guilt resolves through completed action, and an ongoing transfer, by definition, never completes.

Name the identity loss directly instead of paying against it. If you notice the guilt is really about no longer being the provider, protector, or caretaker you spent years being, say that to yourself plainly: *I am not failing to take care of someone. I am grieving the loss of being the kind of person who takes care of this specific someone, and that grief deserves its own attention, separate from my bank account.* Consider where else that identity — provider, caretaker, the person who shows up — can find a legitimate outlet: your children, a friend genuinely in need, a version of generosity that doesn't require staying financially entangled with a marriage that's already over.

Set a firm, calendared date to end any lingering financial tie, and tell someone else that date. Open-ended intentions to "stop soon" rarely resolve on their own, because the guilt driving them doesn't come with a natural expiration. Pick an actual date — thirty days out, sixty at the most — write it down, and tell one trusted person, so there's a real accountability structure around a decision that guilt, left alone, will keep deferring indefinitely.

Use the settlement money for something that concretely builds your new life, on purpose, within a set window. If you're sitting on untouched settlement funds the way the woman in this chapter's second scene was, choose one specific, near-term use for at least a portion of it — the security deposit, the emergency fund, the debt payoff — and act on it within thirty days. The goal isn't to spend it recklessly. It's to interrupt the pattern of treating the money as still somehow contested, unfinished, or not fully, legitimately yours, by using a portion of it the way fully yours money actually gets used.

Notice when guilt is doing attachment's work, and name the attachment instead. If a wave of guilt arrives that feels disproportionate to any actual wrongdoing, ask directly: is this guilt, or is this the ache of a bond that hasn't finished loosening yet? They can feel almost identical from the inside, but they call for different responses. Guilt asks to be resolved through action. Attachment simply asks to be acknowledged, felt, and allowed to fade at its own pace — which it generally will, given enough time and enough distance, without needing a monthly transfer to keep it company.

If you're building a case for an accusation nobody has made, say the fear out loud instead of gathering more evidence for it. Anticipatory guilt rarely responds to more documentation, because the documentation was never actually what the fear was asking for. If you notice yourself preemptively defending against a criticism that hasn't happened, try naming the specific fear directly — *I'm afraid he'll say I'm not doing enough* — to a trusted friend or even to yourself in writing, once, and then deliberately let the folder-building stop. The fear usually loses most of its urgency once it's said in full sentences instead of managed in receipts.

Ask what a genuinely finished obligation actually feels like, and notice the gap. Most people can recall at least one debt, favor, or obligation in their life that resolved cleanly — paid off, thanked, closed, and never thought about again. Compare that felt sense of completion to how the lingering payment or untouched settlement currently feels. If the gap is large, that's useful information: it tells you the obligation you're carrying was never really about the ledger, and no ledger-based action is going to close it the way a genuinely finished obligation closes.

Redirect the identity, not just the money, toward something that has nothing to do with the marriage. If the underlying need is to still be the kind of person who provides and shows up for others, look for a genuinely new outlet unconnected to the ex-partner entirely — volunteering, mentoring, a friend going through a hard season. This channels the real, decent impulse driving the guilt payment into a place where it can actually do good, rather than into a financial tie that mostly just keeps a closed chapter quietly propped open.

Give the fear a specific timeline rather than an indefinite one. If some part of the guilt is genuinely about worrying what will happen to an ex-partner's stability without your help, ask directly how long that worry is realistically warranted — a specific, bounded window tied to an actual circumstance (a job search, a health recovery, a custody transition) rather than an open-ended sense that stopping might always be too soon. A bounded worry is a worry you can actually resolve. An unbounded one just runs indefinitely, regardless of how the actual circumstances change.

The Rule to Remember: the payment you can't stop making is rarely about what you owe your ex-partner — it's about who you're afraid you'll be once you're no longer the one taking care of them, and that fear deserves a better answer than a recurring transfer.

Chapter 3 — The Fortress You Built From the Rubble

Within three months of her divorce being finalized, she had built a system so tight it could survive almost anything — six months of expenses in cash, a spreadsheet tracking every dollar to the cent, automatic transfers locking money away before she could second-guess herself, a hard rule against any purchase over fifty dollars that hadn't been planned at least a week in advance. Her friends, watching from the outside, mostly admired it. She'd been financially blindsided once, during the marriage, by a joint account her ex had quietly drained to cover a gambling habit she hadn't known existed until the balance told her. Nobody was going to catch her flat-footed like that again. The system was, by any conventional measure, an impressive achievement — disciplined, thorough, exactly the kind of financial competence divorce recovery articles tell you to build.

What the system also did, though nobody watching from the outside could quite see it, was slowly close off her life in ways that had nothing to do with financial safety anymore. She turned down a work trip to a conference that would have cost four hundred dollars out of pocket but would likely have led to a promotion, because the spreadsheet flagged it as an unplanned expense and unplanned expenses, in her system, simply didn't get approved, regardless of the return they might generate. She stopped going to dinner with friends unless she'd budgeted for it a week ahead, which meant she often didn't go at all, because spontaneous invitations, by definition, arrived without a week's notice. She'd built a fortress to protect herself from ever being financially blindsided again, and the fortress was working exactly as designed. It just hadn't occurred to her, until a friend finally said something gently over coffee, that a fortress doesn't just keep danger out. It keeps almost everything out, including the parts of a life that were never actually dangerous to begin with.

A different version of the same over-correction showed up for a man whose divorce hadn't involved any betrayal at all — a mutual, sad, entirely amicable parting after growing apart over many years. He hadn't been blindsided the way the woman above had. And still, within a year of the split, he'd become someone who refused to make any financial decision without exhaustively researching every possible outcome first, sometimes for weeks, over purchases that objectively didn't warrant that level of scrutiny — a new mattress, a modest vacation, a subscription service. His adult daughter finally asked him, during one particularly long deliberation over which health insurance plan to select, what he was actually afraid would happen if he just picked one and moved forward. He didn't have a ready answer. When he finally found one, it surprised him: he wasn't afraid of a bad mattress or a wrong health plan specifically. He was afraid, in some deep and largely wordless way, of ever again being a person whose life could be upended by a decision he didn't see coming — and after thirty years of shared decision-making inside a marriage, every decision now felt, unconsciously, like it might carry that same weight, even the small ones that plainly didn't.

A third version surfaces in a domain slightly outside a formal divorce: a woman whose nine-year, unmarried partnership ended abruptly when her partner left with almost no warning, taking with him a level of financial stability she'd quietly, unknowingly come to rely on more than she'd realized.

In the two years that followed, she developed a pattern of refusing any financial risk whatsoever — no investing, not even in a basic retirement account with an employer match she was leaving entirely on the table, because "risk," in any form, had become psychologically indistinguishable from the specific kind of abandonment she'd already survived once. The employer match she declined to claim wasn't a small oversight. Over several years, it represented real, meaningful money left unclaimed, purely because her fortress had been built wide enough to exclude a form of risk that had nothing to do with the actual danger she'd already lived through.

A fourth version of the same pattern shows up in a domain many people don't initially recognize as fortress-building at all: over-insurance. A man two years divorced, whose ex-wife had left the marriage with a large, unforeseen medical bill neither of them had planned for, spent the following two years purchasing every optional insurance product offered to him — extended warranties on appliances, supplemental policies stacked on top of already-comprehensive coverage, a habit of insuring against remote, low-probability risks that had nothing to do with medical debt specifically. His financial advisor, reviewing his accounts, pointed out gently that he was spending several hundred dollars a month insuring against outcomes so unlikely that the premiums alone, over time, cost more than simply covering the rare bad outcome out of pocket would have. He wasn't insuring against medical debt anymore. He was insuring, indiscriminately, against the general feeling of being unprepared again, and insurance products, unlike a fifty-dollar spending rule, are specifically designed to make that indiscriminate feeling easy and profitable for someone else to keep selling to.

What's actually happening

It's worth pausing, before naming the mechanism, on how differently a fortress presents itself compared with the patterns described in the previous two chapters. Where an unfinished ledger or an unnecessary payment tends to read, even to the person doing it, as a sign that something is unresolved, a fortress reads as the opposite: evidence of growth, discipline, hard-won wisdom. That difference in how the pattern presents itself is itself worth understanding, because it means fortress-building is considerably more likely to go unexamined for years, quietly praised by everyone watching, than a pattern that at least announces itself as a problem.

The clearest framework for understanding this pattern comes from psychologist Julian Rotter's foundational research on locus of control — the degree to which a person believes outcomes in their life are determined by their own actions and decisions, as opposed to external forces beyond their influence. Rotter's decades of research established that a person's sense of control isn't fixed; it shifts in response to significant life events, and a sudden, involuntary loss of control — precisely what a divorce, especially a blindsiding one, represents — tends to produce a strong compensatory push toward regaining control wherever it can plausibly be regained. Money, unlike almost every other domain touched by a divorce, is one of the few places where a person genuinely can exert total, unilateral control after the split. There's no ex-spouse to negotiate with anymore, no shared decision-making required, no vote but your own. That makes money an unusually attractive site for a nervous system that has just lost real control elsewhere to over-invest its need for mastery, sometimes far past the point of diminishing returns.

This connects to a broader body of research on control restoration following trauma or significant loss, which has found, consistently, that the drive to reassert control after an involuntary loss of it doesn't calibrate itself automatically to the actual level of risk present in a new situation. It calibrates itself to the intensity of the original loss of control, which means a person blindsided by a genuinely severe betrayal — a drained account, a hidden debt, an affair discovered through a credit card statement — can end up building a level of financial defense wildly disproportionate to the actual risk present in their new, single life, simply because the compensatory drive is responding to the size of the original wound rather than to the size of the current, ordinary decision in front of them. This is precisely what happened to the woman with the fifty-dollar rule: the rule wasn't actually calibrated to protect her from a repeat of what happened. It was calibrated to make the original loss of control feel, retroactively, impossible to have prevented — and no rule, however strict, can actually rewrite the past that thoroughly.

There's a related finding that explains why this pattern is so much harder to see from the inside than fortress-building around any other kind of fear: rigid, hypervigilant control strategies often produce short-term relief that reinforces the strategy even as the strategy's costs accumulate. Every time the woman's spreadsheet caught a small overspend, or the man's exhaustive research prevented a decision he could later point to as "responsible," the behavior received a small hit of genuine relief — a felt sense of safety that operantly reinforces the exact behavior producing it, the same reinforcement mechanism that makes any habit, healthy or not, harder to notice and interrupt the longer it runs. The fortress doesn't feel like a problem from the inside. It feels like evidence of exactly how much the person has learned, how much wiser and more careful they've become — which is part of what makes it so resistant to the gentle, well-meaning pushback of friends who can see, from the outside, what the fortress is actually costing.

Return to the retirement-match story for a moment, because it illustrates a specific and costly blind spot inside this pattern: rigid control strategies built to prevent a repeat of one specific kind of harm frequently fail to distinguish between that specific harm and an entirely unrelated category of risk. The woman's original loss involved abandonment and the collapse of a relied-upon financial partnership — a genuinely relational risk. Declining an employer retirement match involves an entirely different kind of risk, structural and market-based, with essentially no relationship to the mechanism that hurt her the first time. Her fortress, built for one danger, ended up excluding an entirely unrelated category of ordinary, sound financial behavior, simply because "risk" had become, psychologically, a single undifferentiated category rather than the many distinct, differently-weighted categories it actually is. This undifferentiated quality is one of the more reliable signs that a control strategy has tipped from proportionate caution into fortress territory: it stops distinguishing between the specific threat it was built to prevent and every other decision that merely shares a surface resemblance to risk.

One more piece belongs here, drawn from research on psychological flexibility, a concept most closely associated with the work of psychologist Steven Hayes and collaborators in developing acceptance and commitment therapy. This research has found, across many contexts, that rigid, rule-bound behavior — doing the same defensive thing regardless of what a specific situation actually calls for — tends to produce worse long-term outcomes than flexible behavior calibrated to the actual demands of each new circumstance, even when the rigid behavior feels, moment to moment, like the safer choice. A fortress, by definition, applies the same defensive posture to every situation it encounters, including situations, like a work conference or a retirement match, that were never actually dangerous in the first place. The goal this research points toward isn't abandoning caution. It's building a form of caution flexible enough to actually distinguish between real threats and ordinary life, rather than one so uniformly rigid it treats every decision as though it carries the same weight as the one that broke something the first time.

The over-insurance scenario illustrates a related mechanism: the availability heuristic, a well-documented finding from the judgment-and-decision-making research associated with Daniel Kahneman and Amos Tversky, in which people overestimate the probability of an outcome in direct proportion to how vividly and easily they can recall an example of it happening — usually because it happened to them personally, recently, and painfully. A person who has just lived through a genuinely unforeseen financial blow will, for a real, measurable period afterward, systematically overestimate the likelihood of similarly unforeseen blows happening again, in any form, which is precisely what makes remote, low-probability insurance products feel proportionate rather than excessive in the months and years following a divorce. The fear isn't irrational in its origin. It's simply mis-calibrated, running the probability math off one vivid, recent, personally painful data point rather than off the actual, much lower base rate the rest of the evidence would support.

What it costs you

It's worth marking, before the specific costs below, what makes this particular pattern's costs so much harder to add up than an obvious overspending problem would be. A fortress doesn't cost money in any way a bank statement would flag. It costs opportunities that were never taken, relationships that quietly thinned, and growth that simply didn't happen — none of which shows up as a line item anywhere, which is part of why fortress-building can run for years, entirely unexamined, while its costs accumulate in a currency no spreadsheet was ever built to track.

The most direct cost is the one both the woman and the man in this chapter's opening scenes experienced without initially realizing it: real opportunities, foregone not because they were genuinely risky but because they didn't fit a system built for a threat that no longer applies. The conference that could have led to a promotion. The dinners with friends that build exactly the kind of social support divorce recovery research consistently identifies as one of the strongest predictors of successful adjustment. These aren't abstract losses. They're specific, concrete costs to a person's career trajectory, social connection, and quality of life, all incurred in the name of a safety that, in these specific instances, was never actually threatened.

There's a subtler cost to the relationship a person has with their own judgment. A fortress built out of a fear of ever being blindsided again quietly communicates, to the person living inside it, a message that isn't actually true: that their own judgment can't be trusted without an elaborate system of rules to constrain it. This is a particularly cruel cost, because it often lands hardest on people whose judgment was never actually the problem in the original story. The woman whose ex-husband hid a gambling habit wasn't blindsided because her judgment failed. She was blindsided because someone she trusted deliberately concealed information from her — an entirely different failure mode than "I made a bad financial decision." And yet the fortress she built treats her own future decision-making as the primary threat to guard against, which is, on reflection, precisely the wrong lesson to have drawn from what actually happened to her.

There's a cost to new relationships as well, one that shows up with particular force in this specific pattern. A person whose fortress has become rigid enough to exclude spontaneity, flexibility, and shared decision-making can struggle, later, to build the kind of financial partnership a healthy future relationship might eventually call for — not because they're incapable of trust, but because the fortress, by this point, has become load-bearing for their entire sense of stability, and any suggestion of loosening it can trigger a level of anxiety disproportionate to what's actually being asked. This doesn't mean fortress-builders are doomed to permanent isolation. It means the fortress, left unexamined, can quietly become an obstacle to exactly the kind of future the person is otherwise trying to build for themselves.

There's a cost, too, that compounds specifically around retirement and long-term financial growth, illustrated directly by the unmarried woman's declined employer match. Fortress-building, because it treats risk as a single undifferentiated threat rather than a set of distinct, differently-weighted categories, frequently produces exactly the kind of overly conservative long-term investing that leaves real money on the table over a working lifetime — not because the person doesn't understand the math, but because the fortress doesn't distinguish between the emotional risk of trusting a person again and the structural, well-understood risk of a diversified retirement account. Years of an unclaimed employer match, compounding, represents a genuinely significant cost, invisible in any single month but substantial by the time it's finally noticed.

Finally, there's a cost to the process of healing itself. Rigid control, because it produces real short-term relief, can be mistaken — by the person living inside it and by the people around them — for evidence of genuine recovery, when it's often closer to a different kind of unresolved fear, simply rerouted into a more socially acceptable, even admirable-looking form. A person who has built an impressive, disciplined financial fortress is often praised for how well they're doing, which makes it considerably harder for anyone, including the person themselves, to notice that the fortress isn't actually evidence of healing. It's evidence of a wound that hasn't been directly addressed, only very effectively defended against.

There's a final cost worth flagging directly, illustrated by the over-insurance scenario: fortress-building of this kind is genuinely profitable for the institutions selling the products that feed it, which means a person in this pattern is rarely met with a gentle counterweight from the outside. Nobody at an insurance counter is incentivized to say "you probably don't need this." The fortress, once it becomes visible as a pattern a salesperson can recognize and sell into, tends to get reinforced by the market around it rather than questioned, which is part of why this particular version of the pattern can run for years, quietly, without any of the ordinary social feedback that eventually prompts someone to question a fifty-dollar spending rule at a dinner with friends.

Taken as a whole, the four costs above share a structural feature worth saying plainly before turning to the overrides: each one is invisible in the moment it's actually being incurred. Nobody feels the missed promotion the day they decline the conference. Nobody feels the retirement shortfall the month they skip the match. The fortress's costs arrive on a delay, often a long one, which is precisely what makes fortress-building so much easier to sustain than almost any other pattern in this book. A guilt payment shows up on a bank statement every month, visible and countable. A fortress's cost mostly doesn't show up at all, until the day someone finally adds up several years of foregone opportunities and discovers how much safety actually cost.

The overrides

Separate the specific threat from the general category of risk. Write down, precisely, what actually happened to cause the original harm — not "I got hurt financially," but the specific mechanism: concealment, betrayal, a partner acting unilaterally without disclosure. Then, for any new rule your fortress has built, ask directly: does this rule actually guard against that specific mechanism, or does it guard against risk in general, regardless of whether this particular decision shares anything real in common with what happened before? Rules that fail this test are strong candidates for loosening.

The Move: pick one fortress rule and run a small, deliberate experiment against it. Choose the rule costing you the most — the fifty-dollar threshold, the mandatory week of research, the declined retirement match — and deliberately break it once, in a small, bounded, low-stakes way, on purpose. Notice what actually happens. In the overwhelming majority of cases, nothing resembling the original catastrophe occurs, and that lived, felt evidence does more to loosen a rigid rule than any amount of friends telling you, from the outside, that you're being too strict with yourself.

Distinguish relational risk from structural risk, explicitly, every time a new financial decision triggers the fortress reflex. Before declining an opportunity, ask: is this risk dependent on trusting another person the way I was once let down, or is this a structural, well-understood kind of risk — a market, an employer program, an ordinary purchase — that has nothing to do with anyone's honesty or good faith? A retirement match doesn't require trusting anyone the way a joint account with a spouse does. Naming that difference explicitly interrupts the undifferentiated "risk is risk" logic that fortress-building tends to run on.

Reintroduce spontaneity in small, controlled doses rather than all at once. If the fortress has crowded out flexibility entirely, don't try to dismantle it in one dramatic gesture — that tends to trigger exactly the anxiety spike the fortress was built to prevent. Instead, build in a small, pre-approved monthly allowance for genuinely unplanned spending — a modest amount, decided in advance, that exists specifically to be used spontaneously. This gives the nervous system practice tolerating unplanned decisions inside a structure safe enough not to feel like free fall.

Ask what the fortress is protecting you from feeling, not just from losing. Underneath most rigid financial control sits a feeling the person is trying not to have again — helplessness, humiliation, the specific vertigo of not seeing something coming. Naming that feeling directly, even just to yourself, is often more effective at loosening the fortress's grip than any argument about the actual dollar-and-cents math, because the fortress was never really built to manage the math. It was built to manage the feeling.

Recruit a second opinion for decisions the fortress flags as risky, on purpose. Because judgment inside a fortress tends to be systematically over-cautious, build in a habit of running genuinely borderline decisions past one trusted friend or advisor before automatically declining them. This isn't about outsourcing your judgment permanently. It's a temporary calibration check while you're actively working to distinguish real risk from fortress-triggered risk, useful until your own internal sense of the difference becomes more reliable again.

Audit any recurring insurance or protection purchase against its actual, researched probability, not its felt urgency. If you notice a pattern of stacking optional protection products, take one afternoon to look up the real, base-rate likelihood of the outcome each one covers, rather than relying on how urgent the risk feels. The gap between the felt probability, inflated by a recent painful memory, and the actual probability is often the clearest, most concrete evidence available that the availability heuristic, not sound risk management, is currently doing the deciding.

Ask a trusted friend to name your fortress rules back to you, plainly. Because a fortress rarely looks like a problem from the inside, an outside observer who knows you well is often better positioned to spot which of your current financial rules have drifted from proportionate caution into blanket avoidance. Ask directly, and be genuinely willing to hear the answer, even if your first instinct is to defend the rule rather than examine it.

Give the fortress a formal review date, the same way you would any other major financial system. Rules built in crisis rarely get revisited once the crisis has passed, simply because nothing prompts the revisiting. Put a date on the calendar, six or twelve months out, specifically to review every rule the fortress currently runs on, and ask, deliberately, whether each one still earns its place or has quietly outlived the threat it was built to guard against.

The Rule to Remember: the system you built to make sure you're never blindsided again is only doing its job if it can tell the difference between the danger that actually happened and every ordinary decision that merely reminds you of it.

Chapter 4 — The House That Won't Let Go

The divorce settlement had been clear for over two years: she could stay in the house as long as she wanted, buying out her ex-husband's share on a payment schedule both of them had agreed to without much friction. What the settlement hadn't accounted for was that staying in the house would slowly, quietly become the single most expensive decision of her post-divorce financial life, and that she'd keep making it, month after month, long after any practical argument for staying had stopped holding up.

The math, when she finally forced herself to run it honestly, was not close. The mortgage, the maintenance, the property taxes on a four-bedroom house designed for a family of four that now held just her and, every other weekend, her two kids, consumed nearly half her take-home income — money that could have funded a retirement account she hadn't contributed to in three years, or a smaller place in a better location for her actual daily life, or simply breathing room in a budget that had felt tight for longer than she wanted to admit out loud. Every financial advisor she'd ever spoken to, including the one she saw briefly right after the divorce, had said some version of the same thing: the house made sense as a short-term stabilizer for the kids, but at some point, staying stopped being about stability and started being expensive nostalgia dressed up as responsible parenting.

She knew this. She could recite the math back to anyone who asked. And still, every time she got close to actually listing the house, something in her recoiled from the idea with a force that felt entirely disproportionate to a real estate decision. The house wasn't just a house. It was the kitchen where her kids had learned to walk, the yard where every birthday party for a decade had happened, the specific slant of afternoon light in the living room that she'd once, in a much happier year, described to a friend as the reason she fell in love with the place in the first place. Selling it didn't feel like a financial decision. It felt like formally agreeing that the family that had lived there — the one that included her ex-husband, the one she'd once assumed would grow old in this exact house — was actually, finally, permanently over. The mortgage payment wasn't just a mortgage payment anymore. It had become the last remaining structure still actively insisting that the old life hadn't fully ended.

A different version of the same pattern showed up for a man whose divorce hadn't involved a house at all, but a small business he and his ex-wife had built together over nine years — a modest catering company that had, by the time of the divorce, become genuinely profitable, largely due to her client relationships and his operational skill working in tandem. The settlement gave him full ownership; she walked away with a cash payout and no further stake. Three years later, the business was quietly failing, not because the market had changed or because he lacked the skill to run it, but because he'd spent those three years refusing to change almost anything about how it operated — the same menu, the same vendors, the same pricing structure they'd built together, even after several of those choices had stopped making financial sense. A consultant he eventually hired, exasperated after months of watching him reject every proposed change, finally asked him directly what he was actually afraid would happen if he updated the menu. He didn't have an answer ready. When he found one, weeks later, it unsettled him: some part of him believed that changing the business meant admitting that the version of it she'd helped build — the version that represented, in physical form, nine years of a partnership he'd once been genuinely proud of — was gone, and he wasn't ready to be the one who erased it.

A third version, further from the specific mechanics of divorce, surfaces in a widow's story: a woman who, four years after her husband's death, was still driving a car neither of them had ever particularly liked, well past the point it made financial sense to keep repairing it, because it had been the last major purchase they'd made together, decided on together, in a hospital waiting room during what turned out to be one of his final good weeks. Replacing the car, to her, wasn't a financial upgrade. It was retiring the last object that still, physically, connected her daily life to a decision they'd made as a pair.

A fourth version of this pattern shows up in a domain considerably smaller than a house or a business, worth including precisely because of its modest scale: a man, two years divorced, still renewing a country club membership he and his ex-wife had joined together, rarely used it, and could no longer easily justify on his single income, but kept paying for anyway. It wasn't the golf. He barely played. It was that the membership card, sitting in his wallet, still had both their names printed on the household account, an artifact the club's own outdated system had simply never been asked to update, and some part of him had never quite gotten around to correcting it either — not from oversight, he eventually admitted to a friend, but because the card was the last document in his daily possession that still, in black and white, described a household that included two people instead of one.

What's actually happening

It's worth pointing out, before turning to the research directly, why this particular chapter's pattern is so much harder to argue someone out of than the ones before it. A fortress rule or an unnecessary payment can, at least in principle, be debated on financial terms — the math is knowable, even if the feeling resists it. An object tied to a foreclosed future resists that kind of debate entirely, because the actual case for keeping it was never financial to begin with, and no amount of spreadsheet clarity persuades a person to let go of a future they haven't yet finished imagining as lost.

The clearest lens here comes from research on possible selves, developed by psychologists Hazel Markus and Paula Nurius, which describes the mental representations people hold not just of who they currently are, but of who they might become, who they hoped to become, and who they're afraid of becoming. Markus and Nurius's research established that possible selves are powerful motivators of behavior, sometimes more powerful than a person's present, actual circumstances — people will make real, costly decisions in the present specifically to protect or pursue a possible self they've imagined for their future. The house, the business, the car in these three scenes function as physical anchors for a possible self that the divorce, or the death, has technically foreclosed — the self who grew old in that specific house with that specific family, the self who ran that specific business as a shared, ongoing partnership, the self whose marriage included that specific car and the memory attached to it. Letting go of the object doesn't just mean losing a physical asset. It means formally retiring a possible self the person had spent years, sometimes decades, imagining as their actual future — and that retirement, however necessary, is genuinely, measurably harder than an ordinary financial decision, because it's doing identity work disguised as a real estate transaction.

This connects to a broader concept: self-continuity, the sense that one's identity persists meaningfully across time, connecting a person's past to their present and future in a coherent narrative. Psychological research on self-continuity, building on foundational work in identity theory extending back to Erik Erikson's research on identity development, has found that major life disruptions — divorce prominent among them — can genuinely threaten a person's sense of continuous selfhood, producing a felt sense that the self who existed before the disruption and the self existing after it aren't fully, coherently connected. Physical objects tied to the pre-disruption identity — the house, the business, the car — become, in this framework, load-bearing props for continuity itself. Letting go of them can feel, at a level well below conscious reasoning, like severing the thread connecting the person you used to be to the person you currently are, which is a far heavier ask than simply selling a piece of real estate at the right time for sound financial reasons.

Return to the catering business story, because it demonstrates a specific and costly variant of this mechanism: refusing to change rather than refusing to sell. The man never considered giving up the business — by every external measure, he was moving forward, building a new solo chapter as its sole owner. But his refusal to update anything about how it operated reveals that "letting go" isn't only about physical possession. It's about active stewardship, and a business run exactly as it was run during the marriage, unchanged in every particular, functions as a kind of shrine — a structure kept deliberately frozen in the shape it held during a partnership that no longer exists, even while its new sole owner insists, honestly, that he has moved on. This is worth pausing on because it's a version of the erasure fear that can hide even inside decisions that look, from the outside, like clean, decisive moves forward.

There's a related finding here, drawn from research on decision paralysis under identity threat, a body of work within judgment and decision-making research that has documented how decisions carrying heavy identity implications get processed differently, and often far less rationally, than decisions of comparable financial weight that don't touch identity at all. A four-hundred-thousand-dollar house sale and a four-hundred-thousand-dollar investment decision are, in pure financial terms, comparably significant. But the house sale, because it's entangled with possible-self and self-continuity mechanisms the investment decision isn't, gets processed by a very different, much slower, much more conflicted part of the decision-making apparatus — which is precisely why sound financial advice about the house so often fails to move someone who would readily act on equally sound advice about almost anything else. The resistance isn't irrational. It's simply responding to a different, heavier kind of stakes than the balance sheet alone can capture.

The widow's car story clarifies something important about the boundary of this mechanism, worth stating plainly: this pattern is not unique to divorce, and naming that honestly matters, because it means the resistance a divorced person feels toward selling the house isn't a sign of being unusually stuck, or unusually attached to an ex-spouse specifically. It's a predictable response to any major relational loss that leaves physical objects behind as anchors for a possible self that circumstances have foreclosed. The widow isn't failing to grieve her husband by keeping the car. She's doing exactly what the divorced woman with the house and the divorced man with the business are doing — using a physical object to slow down an identity transition that would otherwise feel like it was happening too fast, too completely, all at once.

The country-club membership card adds a useful, smaller-scale illustration of this same mechanism worth spelling out directly: it isn't only large, expensive objects that function as anchors for a foreclosed possible self. Sometimes a small, symbolic document does the same identity work at a fraction of the cost, which is worth knowing because it means this pattern can hide in far more places than the obvious big-ticket ones this chapter has focused on so far. A library card still listing a former spouse's name as an emergency contact, a recipe box never reorganized to remove a shared favorite, a photo left on a nightstand a full year after everything else in the room has changed — the mechanism scales down as readily as it scales up, and it's worth scanning your own life for its smaller, cheaper versions, not just the six-figure ones.

What it costs you

It's worth calling out, before the specific costs below, that this pattern's expense compounds in a particular way the others in this book don't: because the object itself keeps demanding upkeep — a mortgage, an unchanged menu, a repair bill on a car nobody would otherwise keep — the cost isn't a single missed decision. It's a recurring, renewed decision, made again every month, each time re-choosing the old possible self over the resources that could be building the new one.

The most direct cost is financial, and in cases like the house scenario, it's often substantial and ongoing rather than a single missed opportunity. Nearly half a take-home income tied up in a home that no longer matches a person's actual life represents years of foregone retirement contributions, foregone financial flexibility, and foregone opportunities to build the kind of independent financial stability this entire book is arguing for — all sacrificed, month after month, in service of a possible self the actual circumstances no longer support. This cost compounds silently; a missed retirement contribution in year one isn't just that year's contribution lost, it's years of growth on that contribution lost as well, a cost that only becomes fully visible much later, when it's considerably harder to recover from.

There's a cost to the actual people the object was, ostensibly, being preserved for — most visibly the children in the house scenario. Kids generally adapt to a smaller, more financially stable home far better than they adapt to watching a parent visibly, chronically stressed about money in a house that was kept, technically, "for their sake." The preservation instinct, however loving in its intention, can end up producing exactly the instability it was meant to prevent, simply redirected from the physical environment into the emotional and financial atmosphere of the home itself.

There's a business-specific cost worth sitting with in the catering scenario, because it illustrates how this pattern can actively erode the very thing being protected. A business frozen in its old shape, refusing to adapt to a market that has moved on, doesn't stay preserved. It slowly fails — which means the refusal to let go of the old version, intended to honor what was built together, ends up destroying it more thoroughly than an honest, adaptive evolution ever would have. The shrine, left untended in the specific sense of never being allowed to change, doesn't stay a shrine. It becomes a ruin.

There's a cost, too, to the process of actually building the new possible self this reconstruction requires. Every month spent maintaining the old object in its old form is a month not spent actively imagining and investing in who the person is becoming instead — a genuinely important developmental task the research on possible selves identifies as necessary for healthy adaptation after major life disruption. A person who never lets the old possible self fully retire often struggles, correspondingly, to build a vivid, motivating picture of the new one, because so much energy remains tied up maintaining the old.

Finally, there's a cost to the grief itself, similar to the pattern named in Chapter 1. Keeping the object doesn't actually prevent the grief of the loss it represents. It simply extends the timeline over which that grief has to be processed, often at real financial cost, without meaningfully reducing its eventual weight. The house eventually sells, in most of these stories, or the business eventually adapts, or the car eventually gets replaced — the loss doesn't wait forever for permission. Extending the timeline mostly means extending the cost of straddling both a life that's ending and one that hasn't fully begun.

There's a cost specific to the smaller-scale version of this pattern worth stating as well: because a modest recurring cost like a club membership rarely triggers the same scrutiny a house payment does, it can persist far longer, entirely unexamined, simply because it never gets large enough to force a reckoning. A four-hundred-dollar house payment eventually gets audited by circumstance. A ninety-dollar monthly membership often doesn't, which means the smaller version of this pattern can, paradoxically, run for years longer than the larger one, quietly costing real money the whole time, precisely because its size keeps it beneath the threshold that would otherwise prompt someone to ask why it's still there.

Read together, these five costs share a common shape worth naming directly: each one results from confusing the preservation of an object with the preservation of a possible self, when in fact the object was only ever a stand-in, a physical placeholder for something that was already gone the moment the marriage ended. Keeping the house doesn't keep the imagined future alive. It only postpones the moment that future has to be formally, consciously retired — and postponement, in every version of this pattern, turns out to be considerably more expensive than the grief it was meant to soften.

The overrides

Name the possible self the object represents, specifically, before deciding anything about the object itself. Ask directly: what future was I imagining when I first attached myself to this house, this business, this object? Write the answer down in a sentence or two. Naming the possible self you're actually grieving — not "the marriage," but the specific, concrete future you'd pictured — makes it possible to grieve that future honestly, rather than displacing the grief indefinitely onto a decision about square footage or a menu.

The Move: separate the decision to let go from the decision about timing. Much of the paralysis in this pattern comes from treating "should I ever let this go" and "should I let this go right now" as the same question. They aren't. Give yourself explicit permission to answer the first question honestly — yes, eventually, this will need to change — while giving yourself a separate, realistic timeline for the second, rather than forcing yourself into an all-or-nothing decision that keeps producing paralysis because the stakes feel too large to act on all at once.

Build a small, symbolic version of the new possible self before dismantling the object tied to the old one. Before selling the house, take one concrete, felt step toward the future life it represents letting go of — tour a smaller place, price out what the freed-up money could actually build. Before changing the business, run one small pilot of the new approach without fully committing. Giving the new possible self a taste of reality, even in miniature, makes the eventual larger transition feel less like a leap into nothing and more like a step toward something already partly real.

Ask what specifically would be lost if the object changed, separate from what would be lost if the marriage ended. These two losses get fused by default, but they're not actually the same size. The marriage has already ended; that loss is fixed and, by the time you're weighing this decision, already largely absorbed. The object itself — the house, the business, the car — represents a smaller, more specific loss layered on top, and naming that smaller loss explicitly often makes it feel more survivable than the undifferentiated dread of "losing everything at once" that keeping the object is unconsciously trying to prevent.

Involve the people the object is ostensibly being preserved for, honestly, in the actual decision. If children, a business partner, or anyone else is part of the stated reason for holding on, ask them directly, in age-appropriate terms, what they actually need — rather than assuming on their behalf. Kids in particular are frequently far more adaptable, and far less attached to a specific physical structure, than the parent preserving it on their behalf; discovering this directly, rather than assuming it, often removes a significant piece of the resistance.

Set a concrete review date for any object you're not ready to release yet, rather than an indefinite hold. If you're genuinely not ready to sell, change, or replace something right now, that's a legitimate answer — but give it a real expiration, six months or a year out, rather than an open-ended "someday." A review date turns an indefinite avoidance into a bounded decision you'll actually have to revisit, rather than a decision that quietly makes itself by default, year after year, simply because nobody ever forced the question back onto the calendar.

Run a deliberate inventory of the small, cheap anchors, not just the large, expensive ones. Set aside twenty minutes to list every recurring cost, subscription, or membership still connected in any way to the marriage, regardless of how minor. Small anchors are easy to overlook precisely because their size never forces the question, which means they need to be actively hunted for rather than waited on to surface on their own.

Let a trusted friend or advisor name the object's actual financial cost out loud, without editorializing about your

attachment to it. Sometimes the clearest way to see a possible-self anchor for what it is costing you is to hear the plain arithmetic spoken by someone who isn't carrying the emotional weight of the decision. Ask a financial advisor, an accountant, or simply a clear-eyed friend to state the actual cost once, plainly, and let that number sit alongside the harder, less quantifiable case for keeping the object — rather than letting the emotional case argue alone, unopposed, indefinitely.

Write a short, honest eulogy for the possible self the object represents, even if no one else ever reads it. Give the imagined future — the family that would have grown old in that house, the business that would have stayed exactly as it was built — a real, deliberate goodbye in writing, the way you might eulogize a person. This isn't a sentimental exercise for its own sake. Naming a loss explicitly and formally tends to loosen its grip far more effectively than continuing to relate to it only through an object that stands in for it indirectly.

The Rule to Remember: the house, the business, the object you can't quite let go of was never really the thing keeping the old life alive — it was the last place you were

still allowed to visit it, and visiting isn't the same as living there.

Chapter 5 — The Ghost at the Kitchen Table

Two years after her divorce, she stood in a car dealership, ready to buy her first car with only her own name on the loan, and found herself, unprompted, running through a familiar internal script: *he'd say this one's a waste of money, he'd want me to negotiate harder, he'd think the extended warranty is a scam.* The dealership was quiet. Nobody was pressuring her. There was no actual disagreement happening, no real conversation to navigate — just her, alone, in front of a salesperson, silently consulting a person who wasn't there, hadn't been consulted on anything in her life for two years, and would have had, by that point, absolutely no standing to weigh in even if he'd wanted to.

What unsettled her, once she noticed it clearly, wasn't that she remembered his opinions. It was how automatic the process had become — not a conscious decision to ask "what would he think," but a reflex that arrived before she'd had a chance to ask herself what she thought first. She caught herself doing versions of this constantly, in decisions large and small: choosing a grocery store because it was the one they used to go to together, avoiding a particular restaurant because it had been “his pick,” structuring a monthly budget using categories he’d originally set up years earlier, categories that no longer matched her actual life but had never been consciously revisited because revisiting them would have meant admitting the original system was his, not a neutral structure that had simply always existed.

A different version of the same reflex showed up for a man three years into his divorce, in a domain that revealed how deep the pattern could run. He’d remarried, happily, to a woman with entirely different financial habits than his first wife — more spontaneous, less rigidly planned, comfortable with a level of month-to-month flexibility his first marriage had never allowed. And he found himself, repeatedly, silently uncomfortable during his second marriage’s ordinary financial decisions, not because his new wife was doing anything actually risky, but because her approach violated a set of rules his first wife had established, rules he’d internalized so completely that he could no longer distinguish them from his own independent judgment. It took a frank conversation with a therapist, prompted by a fight that had genuinely confused him — he couldn't articulate what was actually wrong with what his new wife had done, only that it felt wrong — for him to realize he'd spent three years unconsciously auditing his second marriage's finances against his first marriage's rulebook, without ever having consciously chosen to keep that rulebook active at all.

A third version of this pattern surfaces for a woman whose long-term, unmarried partnership had ended four years earlier, still catching herself, periodically, reaching for a specific brand of financial caution her ex-partner had modeled so thoroughly during their nine years together that she'd stopped experiencing it as his preference and started experiencing it as simply correct — the objectively right way to handle money, rather than one particular person's particular habit that she had, at some point, unconsciously adopted wholesale and never actually re-examined against her own independent judgment once he was gone.

A fourth version of this pattern shows up in a subtler register: a woman four years divorced who noticed, during a routine conversation with her adult daughter about the daughter's own new apartment, that she'd instinctively begun advising her daughter using her ex-husband's exact negotiating phrases — turns of language she hadn't consciously thought about in years, arriving whole and unbidden, in his cadence rather than her own. It unsettled her less because the advice was bad — it wasn't — and more because she realized, in that moment, that his voice hadn't just shaped her own decisions. It had become part of the voice she was now, unknowingly, passing down to the next generation, a ghost with a longer reach than she'd ever considered.

What's actually happening

This chapter's pattern differs from the previous one in a way worth marking directly: the house or business in Chapter 4 was at least a conscious, visible presence a person could point to and recognize as tied to the marriage. The ghost at the kitchen table is quieter than that, and considerably harder to catch, because it doesn't announce itself as belonging to anyone. It shows up disguised as your own judgment, which means the first task isn't deciding what to do about it — it's noticing it's there at all.

The clearest explanation for this pattern comes from research on habit formation and automaticity, most extensively documented in the work of psychologist Wendy Wood, whose decades of research have established that a striking proportion of daily behavior runs on automatic, cue-triggered processes rather than deliberate, conscious decision-making. Wood's research has shown that habits, once established through sufficient repetition in a stable context, become genuinely independent of the original motivation or relationship that built them — the behavior persists, triggered by familiar cues, even after the reasons for the behavior, or the person who originally modeled it, are no longer present. A years-long marriage is, among other things, an extraordinarily consistent context for habit formation: the same grocery store, the same budgeting categories, the same negotiating instincts, rehearsed and reinforced thousands of times over a decade or more. Those habits don't require the marriage to still be intact in order to keep firing. They only require the original cues — the dealership, the budget spreadsheet, the grocery aisle — to still be present, which they generally are, long after the person who helped install the habits is gone.

This matters because it reframes something that can otherwise feel deeply strange, even a little unsettling: consulting an absent ex-partner's imagined opinion isn't a sign of unresolved attachment or an inability to move on emotionally. It's often simply a habit, running exactly the way habits are designed to run — automatically, below conscious awareness, triggered by a familiar context, regardless of whether the relationship that built the habit still exists. Wood's research is notably reassuring on this point: habits, however automatic, are not permanent or unchangeable. They weaken specifically when their triggering context changes, or when a person deliberately, repeatedly practices a different response in that same context — which offers a genuinely practical path forward, rather than simply waiting for the reflex to fade on its own.

There's a second layer here, drawn from cognitive schema research within psychology, describing the mental frameworks people build over time to organize and interpret experience efficiently, without having to consciously reason through every situation from scratch. A long marriage builds an elaborate financial schema — a shared, internalized sense of what counts as reasonable, what counts as excessive, what a good decision looks like — co-authored by both partners but eventually experienced, by each of them, as simply "how things are" rather than as a jointly constructed, negotiable framework. This is precisely what happened to the remarried man: his first marriage's financial schema had become so thoroughly internalized that he could no longer distinguish it from his own independent judgment, which is exactly what a well-established schema is designed to feel like from the inside. Schemas don't announce themselves as constructed. They present themselves as reality, which is part of why the man needed an outside perspective — a therapist, in his case — to even notice the schema was there at all, let alone that it belonged to a specific person and a specific, now-ended relationship rather than to objective financial truth.

The unmarried woman's story adds an important piece here, because it demonstrates that the mechanism doesn't require the formal weight of a marriage to install itself this thoroughly. Nine years of consistent modeling, inside a partnership serious enough to structure a daily life around, was sufficient to build a schema every bit as durable and every bit as invisible as the ones built inside the two marriages described above. Put plainly: the depth of the schema tracks the depth and duration of the shared life, not the legal status of the relationship that built it, which means readers navigating the end of a long-term unmarried partnership shouldn't assume this particular mechanism applies to them any less thoroughly just because no marriage certificate was ever involved.

One more piece connects back to the self-expansion research introduced in Chapter 1. If a partner's traits and preferences genuinely become cognitively fused with a person's own sense of self during a long relationship, it follows naturally that the partner's financial opinions would come to feel, from the inside, indistinguishable from one's own independently formed judgment. The "ghost" at the kitchen table isn't really haunting anyone in a supernatural sense. It's a set of internalized preferences that were, for years, genuinely part of how the self operated, and separating them back out into "this was actually his opinion, not mine" is real, deliberate psychological work — not something that happens automatically just because the relationship legally ended.

The advice-to-her-daughter scene points to a further layer, connected to Albert Bandura's observational-learning research introduced later in this book but relevant here as well: modeled behavior doesn't stay contained to the person who first absorbed it. A financial schema, once installed, tends to get transmitted onward to anyone who watches it in action closely enough and often enough — a child, in this case, receiving advice built from a marriage that ended before the advice was ever consciously chosen to be passed on. This isn't cause for alarm; most of what any parent passes down was absorbed the same unconscious way from someone else first. But it's a further reason this chapter's overrides matter beyond the individual doing the work: an unexamined ghost doesn't only shape one person's decisions. Left unexamined long enough, it can quietly become the next generation's starting schema too.

What it costs you

It's worth flagging, before the specific costs below, that this pattern's expense is uniquely hard to notice while it's happening, precisely because a habit running on autopilot doesn't feel like a decision at all. The costs that follow aren't the result of choosing wrong. They're the result of not knowing a choice was ever available.

The most direct cost is a subtle but persistent loss of authentic financial autonomy — years spent making decisions filtered through a rulebook that was never fully, consciously chosen, and that may no longer serve a life that has changed substantially since the rulebook was written. The woman avoiding a restaurant because it was "his pick" isn't making a decision based on her actual current preferences. She's outsourcing the decision to a schema that's years out of date, built by and for a partnership that no longer exists, which means her actual, current life is being organized, in small but cumulative ways, by a person who no longer has any legitimate role in organizing it.

There's a cost that shows up specifically in new relationships, illustrated directly by the remarried man's story: an old, unexamined financial schema can create real friction in a new partnership, not because the new partner is doing anything actually wrong, but because their entirely reasonable habits are being measured against an invisible, inherited rulebook they were never told existed and have no way of knowing they're being judged against. This is a genuinely unfair position to put a new partner in, however unintentionally, and it can produce exactly the kind of confusing, hard-to-name conflict the man experienced — friction that neither party can fully articulate, because one of them is arguing from a rulebook the other doesn't even know is in the room.

There's a cost to the reconstruction process itself, the central work this entire book is arguing for. A financial identity that's still, unconsciously, running large portions of an ex-partner's schema isn't actually a new, independently built identity, however much it might look like one from the outside. It's closer to a modified version of the old joint identity, missing its second author but still operating according to rules that author helped write. Real reconstruction requires actually noticing which parts of a current financial life reflect genuine, independently held values, and which parts are simply habit residue from a relationship that's already over — a distinction that takes real, deliberate attention to draw, because the schema, as noted above, doesn't announce itself as inherited.

There's a cost, too, to a person's confidence in their own judgment, similar to but distinct from the cost named in Chapter 1. Someone who keeps discovering, months or years after a divorce, that a "personal" financial preference actually originated with an ex-partner can develop a nagging uncertainty about which of their remaining preferences are genuinely their own — a kind of retroactive doubt that, left unaddressed, can generalize into a broader hesitancy to trust any of their own financial instincts, even the ones that were never actually borrowed in the first place.

Finally, there's a cost to genuinely moving forward, in the fullest sense this book has been describing since Chapter 1. A financial identity haunted by an unexamined ghost isn't yet a fully individual one, no matter how many months or years have passed since the divorce, and no matter how much practical, independent competence has genuinely been built in other areas. The habits running underneath the surface don't update themselves just because time has passed. They update only through the kind of deliberate, active noticing the overrides below are built to prompt.

There's a final cost worth saying, specific to the transmission risk illustrated above: a ghost passed on to a child arrives with none of the context that might let the child later recognize it as inherited rather than universal. The daughter in this scene received genuinely useful negotiating language, but received it without the surrounding story — without knowing it originated in a marriage that ended, shaped by one specific man's particular style rather than by some neutral, universally correct approach to negotiating. Without that context, she inherits not just the advice but the same invisible, unexamined-schema problem her mother has spent years trying to untangle, simply one generation further removed from its origin.

It's worth adding, before the overrides, one last observation about why this particular chapter's pattern tends to be the slowest of the nine to fully resolve: unlike a fortress rule or a guilt payment, a ghost doesn't announce its presence through discomfort. It announces itself, if at all, through a vague, hard-to-place sense that something in a decision doesn't quite feel like your own — a feeling easy to dismiss, easy to override with confidence, easy to mistake for simple certainty rather than inherited certainty. That subtlety is precisely why the overrides below lean so heavily on outside perspective rather than internal reflection alone; a ghost is, almost by definition, harder to spot from the inside than from anywhere else.

Considered together, every cost in this chapter traces back to the same root: a schema that presents itself as neutral, universal common sense is far more durable, and far more dangerous to an authentic reconstruction, than a schema a person consciously recognizes as inherited and chooses to keep or discard on its own merits. The work ahead isn't rejecting everything the marriage taught. Plenty of it may genuinely still serve you well. The work is making the choice conscious, so that whatever survives the audit survives because it's actually yours, not because nobody ever thought to ask.

The overrides

Run a genuine second opinion, out loud, against the reflexive first one. The next time you notice yourself silently consulting an ex-partner's imagined opinion, pause and ask, explicitly: setting aside what he or she would have said, what do I actually think about this, based on my own current life, my own current priorities, my own current situation? This isn't about rejecting every inherited preference automatically — some of them may genuinely still serve you well. It's about making sure the preference survives on its own merits, examined fresh, rather than surviving purely on inertia.

The Move: physically change one cue tied to a strong financial habit, on purpose. Because habits are triggered by context, changing the context is one of the most effective ways to interrupt an automatic response. Switch grocery stores, restructure your budget categories from scratch rather than editing an inherited template, choose a genuinely new restaurant instead of avoiding an old shared one. The goal isn't permanent avoidance of anything associated with the marriage — it's giving yourself enough of a break from the old triggering cues that a new, independently chosen habit actually has room to form in their place.

Audit your financial rules for authorship, once, deliberately. Set aside real time to go through your current financial habits and ask, plainly, of each one: did I choose this, or did I inherit this? You won't be able to answer with total certainty for every single habit, and that's fine — the value is in the practice of asking the question at all, which tends to surface at least a few genuine surprises, rules you'd stopped questioning because they'd started to feel like simply how things are, the same way the remarried man's first-marriage schema had.

Give a new partner, or a new financial chapter, an actual clean slate rather than an inherited rulebook. If you're building a new relationship, financial or otherwise, make a deliberate effort to build its financial norms fresh, discussed openly with the new partner, rather than importing an old rulebook unconsciously and measuring the new relationship against it without ever naming that the rulebook exists. This is a genuine act of fairness to whoever you're building the new chapter with — they deserve to be evaluated on their own terms, not against a ghost they never met.

Notice when discomfort in a new financial situation feels like judgment rather than preference. If a new partner's, or your own new, financial decision produces a reaction that feels more like moral disapproval than simple difference of taste, treat that as a signal worth investigating. Preferences feel like "I'd rather do it differently." Inherited schema violations tend to feel like "that's wrong," even when there's no actual objective wrongness involved — and that specific flavor of reaction is often the clearest available marker that a ghost, rather than your own current judgment, is the one actually talking.

Practice the new response deliberately, more than once, rather than expecting one insight to dissolve years of habit. Because habits weaken through repeated practice of an alternative response rather than through a single moment of realization, expect to catch and correct the same reflex multiple times before it genuinely fades. This isn't a sign the work isn't taking. It's simply how habit change actually works, according to the research this whole chapter has been drawing on, and expecting instant, permanent change after one moment of noticing is a setup for unnecessary discouragement.

When you catch yourself passing inherited advice to someone else, add the context out loud. If you notice yourself teaching a child, a friend, or anyone else a financial habit or phrase that actually originated with an ex-partner, say so directly — "I learned this from someone I was married to, and it's served me well, but you should decide for yourself if it fits you." This small act of attribution does real work: it turns an invisible, universally-presented rule into a visible, examinable one, giving the next person the chance to keep it, adapt it, or discard it on their own terms rather than inheriting it as unquestioned fact the way you may have.

Build one new, deliberately chosen ritual to replace an inherited one, rather than leaving the space empty. Habits that get interrupted don't simply vanish — the space they occupied tends to get filled by something, often by default rather than by choice. If you're deliberately breaking an inherited financial habit, decide in advance what will take its place, chosen on purpose, so the old cue doesn't simply relapse into the old response out of sheer absence of an alternative.

Ask a close friend which of your financial phrases sound like someone else. People who know you well from before and after the marriage are often better positioned than you are to notice when a particular turn of phrase, negotiating style, or financial rule sounds distinctly like your ex-partner rather than like you. Ask directly, and treat the answer as useful data rather than criticism — an outside ear frequently catches an inherited schema faster than internal reflection alone ever will.

The Rule to Remember: the opinion you're still consulting at the dealership, the grocery store, the budget spreadsheet belongs to someone who no longer has a seat at your table — the seat is still there because you haven't yet noticed you're the one keeping it set.

Chapter 6 — The Fairness You Can't Stop Litigating

Eighteen months after the divorce, she could still recite the settlement from memory, down to individual line items, and she still, on a bad night, ran the numbers again — not because anything about the settlement had changed, but because some part of her kept returning to it the way a tongue keeps returning to a sore tooth, checking, obsessively, whether it still hurt. Her ex-husband had kept the retirement account he'd built during the eleven years they were together, offset by her keeping a larger share of equity in the house. On paper, both attorneys and the mediator had agreed, it was a genuinely fair, roughly equal split. And still, at least once a month, usually late at night, she found herself recalculating whether it had actually been fair — whether the house equity, which would take years to realize as actual cash, was really an equivalent trade for a retirement account that was, at that very moment, quietly compounding somewhere she couldn't see or touch.

What made the recalculating particularly exhausting, once she noticed the pattern clearly, was that it never actually resolved anything. She'd run the numbers, conclude, again, that the split had been reasonable, feel briefly settled, and then find herself running them again three weeks later, as though some part of her needed the math to come out differently this time, or needed to be reassured all over again that she hadn't been quietly cheated by a process she'd fully participated in and formally agreed to.

A different version of the same pattern showed up between two adult siblings, not ex-spouses, in a story worth including because it clarifies how far this mechanism extends beyond a marriage's direct terms. Their parents' divorce, decades earlier, had left one sibling living primarily with their financially comfortable father and one living primarily with their financially strained mother — an arrangement neither child had chosen, made when they were far too young to have any say in it. Thirty years later, as adults with entirely separate financial lives, the sibling who'd grown up with less money still, on some level, tracked what he perceived as a lifetime of unequal treatment, bringing it up, obliquely, at family gatherings decades after either parent had any capacity to change what had already happened. He wasn't litigating his own divorce. He was still, unconsciously, litigating his parents' divorce, using a comparison that had calcified in childhood and never gotten a fair hearing since.

A third version surfaces between two former business partners whose company dissolved alongside their romantic relationship — an unmarried couple who'd built a small design studio together over six years, splitting equally on paper when the relationship and the business ended simultaneously. Two years later, one of them was still quietly tracking every new client the other picked up, every visible sign of professional success, running an informal ledger of who had "really" earned more of the studio's original success and whether the equal split had, in retrospect, actually reflected that. The business was over. The comparison wasn't.

A fourth version of this pattern surfaces years further out, between two ex-spouses whose divorce had been finalized nearly a decade earlier, both now remarried, both financially comfortable by any reasonable measure. What kept the equity litigation alive, long after either of them had any practical reason to revisit it, was a single asset neither had thought to fully resolve at the time: a small parcel of land, inherited by one of them mid-marriage and left, by oversight rather than design, out of the original settlement's careful accounting. A decade later, a chance conversation at their daughter's graduation surfaced the omission, and what should have been a simple, easily correctable oversight instead reopened, in both of their minds, a fairness calculation neither had actively thought about in years — proof that even a genuinely well-negotiated settlement can leave a single loose thread capable of pulling an entire dormant equity ledger back into active use, a decade after both parties believed the account was closed for good.

What's actually happening

It's worth noting, before turning to the framework itself, what makes this chapter's pattern distinct from the guilt described in Chapter 2, even though both can look, from the outside, like an inability to let a settled matter rest. Guilt asks whether you did right by someone else. The fairness litigation this chapter describes asks something colder and more self-directed: whether you were done right by. That's a different question, chasing a different kind of resolution, and it responds to a different set of overrides than the ones that worked for guilt.

The clearest framework here comes from equity theory, developed by psychologist J. Stacy Adams, which describes how people evaluate fairness not through an absolute assessment of what they received, but through a ratio: what they put into a relationship or exchange relative to what they got out of it, compared against the same ratio for the other party involved. Adams's research established that perceived inequity — a felt sense that the input-to-outcome ratio is unbalanced, even when both parties agreed to the terms — produces genuine, persistent psychological distress, and that distress tends to drive continued mental litigation of the perceived imbalance long after any practical opportunity to actually change it has passed. This matters directly here, because a divorce settlement is, among other things, an equity calculation performed under enormous emotional strain, often without full clarity about the actual long-term value of what's being traded — years of a marriage's worth of contributions, some financial and easily quantified, some invisible and much harder to price, being resolved into a single set of terms that has to somehow represent fairness for an entire shared life. It's genuinely difficult to feel settled about an equity calculation that complex, which helps explain why the recalculating in the opening scene never actually produces lasting resolution — the ratio being compared was never fully knowable to begin with, which means no amount of re-running the numbers will ever produce the clean, certain verdict the recalculating is unconsciously searching for.

This connects directly to Leon Festinger's foundational research on social comparison, which established that people evaluate their own outcomes largely through comparison with relevant others, rather than through any absolute, external standard. An ex-spouse is, for obvious reasons, one of the most psychologically available and relevant comparison points a person will ever have — someone whose financial trajectory remains, in many cases, at least partially visible for years after a divorce, through shared friends, shared children, or simple public information, providing a constant, involuntary stream of new comparison data that keeps the equity calculation perpetually reopened rather than allowing it to settle. This is part of what distinguishes divorce-related equity litigation from most other kinds: the comparison target rarely disappears from view the way a stranger or a one-time transaction partner would. He's still there, at pickup, at graduations, sometimes visible on social media, each sighting a small, fresh data point the equity-checking mechanism can't help but process.

The sibling story adds an important layer: equity comparisons initiated by a divorce don't confine themselves to the two people who were actually married. Children of divorce frequently develop their own equity ledgers, tracking perceived fairness in how the divorce's consequences were distributed between them, and those ledgers, built in childhood without the reasoning capacity or full information an adult would have, can persist for decades, essentially unexamined, because nobody ever framed them as a legitimate thing to bring up and resolve directly. The sibling in this story isn't being petty or ungrateful. He's running a genuinely human equity comparison, using data collected as a child, about a decision he had no part in making and no power to change — which makes the comparison especially hard to resolve, since there's no realistic path to renegotiating terms that were set thirty years ago by people who are no longer positioned, practically or emotionally, to revisit them.

There's a further piece here, drawn from research on rumination — the tendency to engage in repetitive, unproductive dwelling on a distressing topic — most extensively studied by psychologist Susan Nolen-Hoeksema across several decades of research into how rumination differs from productive problem-solving. Nolen-Hoeksema's work found that rumination, unlike genuine reflection aimed at resolving a problem, tends to be self-perpetuating precisely because it doesn't lead anywhere — it revisits the same distressing material repeatedly without generating new information or a path to actual resolution, which describes with real precision what's happening every time the woman in the opening scene reruns numbers that have already been settled by a legally binding agreement. The recalculating isn't problem-solving. There's no new problem to solve; the settlement is finished. It's rumination wearing the clothes of financial diligence, which is part of why it feels so productive in the moment and accomplishes so little across the months it continues.

The decade-later land parcel illustrates a related finding: equity ledgers that appear fully closed are often better described as dormant rather than resolved, because the underlying sense of an unequal ratio never actually got a genuine, felt resolution — it simply stopped having new fuel to run on. A single overlooked detail, surfacing years later, can reactivate the entire mechanism almost instantly, precisely because the original distress was never actually metabolized, only starved of the ongoing visibility that had been keeping it active. This is worth knowing in advance, because it means genuine closure requires more than simply letting a comparison go quiet through lack of new information. It requires actually resolving the felt sense of the ratio itself, which the overrides below are built to help with directly.

What it costs you

There's a cost worth pointing out before the specific ones below, distinct from every other chapter in this book: this is the only pattern here where the triggering document is, by design, permanent and unchangeable. A guilt payment can be stopped. A fortress rule can be loosened. A ghost's opinion can be examined and set aside. A signed, legally binding settlement, by contrast, cannot be renegotiated on a whim, which means the recalculating this chapter describes is chasing a resolution that isn't just difficult to reach — it's structurally unavailable, no matter how many times the numbers get rerun.

The most immediate cost is the one Nolen-Hoeksema's research would predict directly: genuine, measurable psychological distress, recurring on a loop, disproportionate to any actual, remaining decision that needs to be made. The late-night recalculating doesn't produce a better outcome. It produces the same conclusion, arrived at repeatedly, at real emotional cost each time, with nothing to show for the expenditure except a worse night's sleep and a morning spent slightly more depleted than it needed to be.

There's a relationship cost, both to co-parenting arrangements where an ex-spouse remains a regular presence, and to new relationships forming alongside the litigation. A person still actively running an equity ledger against an ex-partner tends to bring a subtle vigilance into every subsequent interaction with them — a watchfulness that can read, to children observing it, as ongoing hostility, even when both parents believe they're being appropriately civil on the surface. Co-parenting research consistently identifies ongoing parental conflict, rather than divorce itself, as the more significant predictor of difficulty for children navigating a split, and unresolved equity litigation is a genuinely common, largely invisible source of exactly that ongoing friction.

There's a cost that shows up specifically in how a person relates to their own new financial life, illustrated by the former design-studio partners. Time spent tracking an ex-partner's professional or financial trajectory is time and attention not spent building one's own — a genuinely finite resource of focus and energy that equity litigation quietly siphons away from the actual, present-tense work of reconstruction this whole book is describing. The former business partner tracking every new client his ex-partner landed wasn't, in that same period, investing equivalent energy into growing his own client base; the comparison had become a substitute for building, rather than a spur toward it.

There's a generational cost worth pausing on directly, drawn from the sibling story: unresolved equity litigation from a divorce doesn't necessarily stay contained to the two people who were married. It can propagate into the next generation's relationships with each other, quietly shaping sibling dynamics, family gatherings, and inheritance expectations for decades, long after the original divorce has faded from most people's active memory. This is a cost worth taking seriously precisely because it's so rarely discussed in divorce literature focused narrowly on the divorcing couple themselves.

Finally, there's a cost to the sense of closure this entire book has been arguing is necessary for genuine reconstruction. An equity ledger that never gets formally closed keeps a person psychologically tethered to a comparison that will, by its nature, never resolve cleanly, because a truly fair accounting of an entire shared marriage was never actually calculable to begin with, no matter how many times the numbers get rerun. Waiting for that calculation to finally feel settled is waiting for something the calculation itself was never capable of providing.

There's a final cost illustrated by the land-parcel story worth spelling out honestly: dormant equity ledgers have a way of resurfacing at exactly the moments a family most needs both former spouses functioning well together — a graduation, a wedding, a medical emergency involving a shared child. The cost of an unresolved ratio isn't evenly distributed across the calendar. It concentrates, disproportionately, at precisely the high-stakes family moments where both parties can least afford a decade-old fairness dispute reopening in real time, in front of the people the divorce was, in every other respect, supposed to have long since stopped affecting.

Taken together, every cost named in this chapter shares a single origin worth stating plainly: a settlement is a document, but fairness is a feeling, and documents can be finished in an afternoon in a way feelings simply cannot. The recalculating this chapter describes isn't a failure to accept the paperwork. It's the ordinary, human difficulty of feeling settled about something that was never, in the end, fully calculable — and recognizing that gap for what it is tends to matter more than any single override below, because it reframes the entire project from "solve the math" to "make peace with an answer the math was never going to fully provide."

The overrides

Name the specific comparison driving the rumination, then ask if it's still actionable. The next time you catch yourself recalculating a settled agreement, pause and ask directly: is there an actual decision still pending here, or am I simply re-litigating something that's already legally, practically finished? If nothing is actually pending, the recalculating isn't due diligence. It's rumination, and naming it as rumination — rather than as prudent financial review — is often enough to interrupt the loop, at least partially, in the moment it's happening.

The Move: write the settlement's logic down once, in full, and refer back to the document instead of re-deriving it from memory. Create a single, clear record of why the settlement was structured the way it was — the reasoning behind each major trade-off, the actual professional advice you received at the time. When the recalculating urge strikes, read the document instead of running the numbers again from scratch. This interrupts the self-perpetuating nature of rumination by giving the mind a finished answer to return to, rather than an open question to keep re-solving.

Set a hard limit on how much visibility you allow into an ex-partner's ongoing financial life, where you have any real control over it. Muting or limiting social media, asking mutual friends not to relay financial updates, declining to ask pointed questions at pickups or family events — none of this is about denial. It's about removing unnecessary fuel from a comparison mechanism that, per Festinger's research, runs on exactly this kind of ongoing visibility, and that tends to quiet down considerably once the steady stream of new comparison data slows down.

If the comparison predates your own marriage — inherited from childhood, from parents' divorce — name that origin explicitly. The sibling in this chapter's story would likely find real relief simply in recognizing, out loud, that he's carrying a comparison built when he was a child, using information and reasoning he no longer fully has access to or agrees with as an adult. Naming a ledger as inherited rather than current often reduces its emotional charge considerably, even when the underlying facts haven't changed at all.

Redirect the energy spent tracking an ex-partner's trajectory into a concrete, comparable investment in your own. If you notice real time going into monitoring an ex-spouse's or ex-partner's financial or professional progress, choose one specific, comparable action to invest in your own trajectory instead — updating a resume, researching a career move, actually building the retirement account you have full control over now. This isn't about ignoring genuine unfairness where it exists. It's about making sure your finite attention builds something rather than only measures something.

Consider a single, formal closing ritual for the equity question, rather than an endless informal one. Some people find real value in one deliberate, bounded act of closure — a final conversation with a financial advisor confirming the settlement was reasonable, a letter written and never sent, a specific date marked as "the day I stop recalculating this." A bounded ritual, chosen once and treated as final, tends to succeed where an open-ended intention to "just let it go eventually" generally doesn't, because rumination, left without a formal stopping point, rarely provides one on its own.

Resolve loose threads proactively, rather than waiting for them to resurface at a bad moment. If you know of a genuinely unresolved detail from the original settlement — an overlooked asset, an ambiguous clause, a conversation that never fully happened — address it deliberately, on neutral ground, before a family event forces the issue. A loose thread handled on your own timeline, calmly, costs far less than the same thread unraveling in front of a graduating daughter who never asked to referee it.

Distinguish a genuinely reopened question from a familiar emotional echo. Not every late-night recalculation is pure rumination; occasionally a genuinely new piece of information does surface, the way the overlooked land parcel did a decade later. Before dismissing every recalculation as unproductive, ask honestly: is there real, new information here, or does this feel exactly like the last dozen times I ran these same numbers with nothing new to show for it? The former deserves real attention. The latter deserves the overrides above.

If a genuinely new fact surfaces, resolve it once, formally, rather than letting it reopen the whole ledger. When a real oversight comes to light, the way the land parcel did a decade later, handle it as its own bounded, addressable issue — a conversation, a document, a single correction — rather than allowing it to drag the entire settlement back into active litigation. A specific fix for a specific gap keeps the reopened thread from metastasizing into a full renegotiation of a decision that was, in every other respect, already settled and done.

The Rule to Remember: a settlement that was fair enough to sign doesn't become unfair every time you run the numbers again at midnight — the recalculating was never really checking the math, it was checking whether the loss still hurts, and it always will, for a while, no matter what the spreadsheet says.

Chapter 7 — The Name on the New Account

The first time she filled out a form asking for "employment" and "income" with no space for a second applicant, she stared at it for longer than the form warranted. It was a routine lease application, nothing unusual about it. But something about seeing her own name occupy every line that used to require two — her income alone, her credit history alone, her employment alone standing as the entire application rather than half of one — produced a small, specific jolt of something she couldn't immediately name. It wasn't fear, exactly. It was closer to the feeling of stepping onto a stage she hadn't rehearsed for, discovering, mid-performance, that she actually knew her lines.

She got the apartment. The application went through cleanly, her income alone was more than sufficient, her credit history solid. And in the weeks that followed, she noticed something she hadn't expected: a small, quiet confidence starting to accumulate, decision by decision, each one completed successfully and entirely on her own. Choosing an internet provider without a second opinion. Negotiating her own salary at a performance review for the first time in years without running the number past anyone first. Setting up a retirement account with only her name on the beneficiary line, her own risk tolerance, her own timeline. None of these were large decisions individually. But each one deposited something into an account that had been running dangerously low since the divorce — evidence, accumulated one small proof at a time, that the person filling out these forms was, in fact, capable of running her own financial life competently, without a co-signer, without a silent consultation, without the apparatus of a partnership she no longer had.

A different version of this same reconstruction showed up for a man who'd spent the first year after his divorce deeply unsettled by a specific, recurring thought: that his ex-wife had always been "the financial one" in the marriage, better with numbers, more naturally organized, and that he was now facing a financial life he wasn't equipped to run alone. He avoided his own bank statements for months, deferred every financial decision as long as possible, and generally behaved as though a genuine skill deficit was the core problem he was facing. What eventually shifted things wasn't a course or a book on personal finance — he'd tried both, without much lasting effect. It was a single afternoon, six months in, spent doing his own taxes for the first time in fifteen years, expecting to fail at it, and discovering, with real surprise, that he understood the forms perfectly well, that the work wasn't actually beyond him, that "the financial one" designation had described a division of labor inside a marriage, not an accurate measure of his own individual capability. He'd simply never had the occasion to test it, because for fifteen years, testing it had never been necessary.

A third version surfaces for a woman navigating the end of a long unmarried partnership, discovering, in the process of building her first fully independent financial identity in her early forties, that she genuinely didn't know what her own individual risk tolerance was, separate from the compromise position she and her ex-partner had settled on together over nine years. Building her first solo investment portfolio required, before any actual investing could happen, a strange and unexpectedly clarifying process of figuring out what she actually wanted, independent of what a negotiated partnership had settled on — a question she realized, with some surprise, she had genuinely never had to answer for herself as an adult.

What's actually happening

This chapter marks a turn worth calling out directly, because the first six chapters described patterns that needed interrupting, while this one describes something closer to a deficit that needs actively filling. That distinction matters for how you read what follows: the work here isn't catching a reflex before it fires, the way the earlier chapters largely asked. It's the slower, more constructive work of building something that may genuinely not exist yet, brick by brick, through repeated action rather than through a single moment of noticing.

The clearest framework for understanding this reconstruction comes from psychologist Albert Bandura's extensive research on self-efficacy — a person's belief in their own capacity to execute the actions required to produce a specific outcome. Bandura's research, spanning decades, identified mastery experiences — direct, successful, personally executed accomplishment of a task — as the single most powerful source of genuine self-efficacy, considerably more effective than verbal encouragement, observing someone else succeed, or simply being told a skill deficit doesn't actually exist. This explains precisely why the man's tax-filing afternoon did more for his financial confidence than months of avoidance-driven anxiety or well-meaning reassurance from friends ever could. Self-efficacy isn't built by being told you're capable. It's built by direct, personal, successful execution — which means the reconstruction this entire book has been describing can't actually be accomplished through reading, planning, or reassurance alone. It requires actual, accumulated action, each successfully completed task depositing a small, durable increment of genuine confidence that no amount of external encouragement can substitute for.

This matters enormously for understanding why the lease application produced such an outsized emotional response relative to its actual, modest financial stakes. It wasn't really about the apartment. It was a mastery experience — a small, complete, successfully executed act of independent financial competence — and Bandura's research would predict exactly the kind of quiet confidence accumulation the woman noticed afterward, because each subsequent independent decision functioned as another mastery experience, building on the last, gradually constructing a self-efficacy that the marriage's joint decision-making structure had never required her to build before.

There's a second layer here, connecting back to the discussion of identity in earlier chapters: the man's "financial one" story illustrates how thoroughly a marriage's internal division of labor can be mistaken, by both partners, for an accurate reflection of individual capability, rather than what it actually is — an efficient, negotiated allocation of tasks between two people, chosen for reasons that often have as much to do with interest, time, and early habit as with any real difference in underlying skill. Research on couples and household division of labor, extending across both domestic and financial tasks, has consistently found that these divisions, once established, tend to calcify quickly and get read by both partners as reflecting fixed, inherent aptitude, even when the actual origin was closer to circumstance — whoever happened to take on the task first, whoever had more time in a particular season of the marriage, whoever simply expressed slightly more initial interest. The label "the financial one" wasn't a diagnosis. It was a historical accident that hardened into an identity, for both partners, well past the point where it accurately described anything real about either person's actual capability.

The third scenario adds an important dimension: reconstruction after a long relationship isn't only about proving you can execute known tasks alone. It sometimes requires discovering preferences and values that never had occasion to exist as independent positions in the first place, because they were always negotiated, from the start, as part of a partnership. Research on preference construction, a body of work within decision science examining how people's stated preferences are often actively built in the moment of being asked, rather than retrieved from some pre-existing, fully formed internal position, is directly relevant here. The unmarried woman's uncertainty about her own risk tolerance wasn't a gap in self-knowledge she'd simply failed to notice before. It's likely that an independently held risk tolerance, separate from the negotiated compromise position, had genuinely never existed as a distinct thing to know, because it had never once been asked to exist independently during nine years of partnership. Building it now isn't remembering something forgotten. It's constructing something for the first time — which is a slower, and in some ways more interesting, process than simple recall, and worth understanding as such rather than expecting it to arrive instantly.

A fourth scenario clarifies how far self-efficacy building has to travel for some readers before it can even begin: a woman in her late thirties, married directly out of college, discovered during her divorce that she had never once, as an independent adult, held a bank account, applied for credit, or made a purchase over a hundred dollars without her husband's direct involvement. She wasn't navigating a partial gap in confidence the way the man doing his own taxes for the first time in fifteen years was. She was starting, in her financial life, from a position closer to the one she'd occupied at eighteen, before the marriage had ever begun, except now carrying the added weight of feeling that a woman her age should already know how to do all of this. Her path through Bandura's mastery-experience framework simply had to start further back, with smaller, more foundational tasks, and required a specific act of self-compassion the other scenarios in this chapter didn't quite call for: releasing the expectation that competence at her age should have arrived automatically, rather than needing to be built, deliberately, starting now.

There's a final piece worth sitting with, returning to Bandura's broader body of work: self-efficacy, once built through genuine mastery experience, tends to generalize — meaning confidence built through successfully completing one financial task tends to spill over, measurably, into confidence approaching other, related tasks, even ones that haven't been directly tested yet. This is the mechanism underneath the quiet, compounding confidence the woman in the opening scene described noticing. It wasn't that each individual task was, in itself, transformative. It's that the accumulated pattern of successful, independent execution began to genuinely change her underlying belief about her own capability across the board — precisely the shift this entire book is arguing the reconstruction process ultimately depends on.

What it costs you

It's worth stating, before the specific costs below, what makes inaction in this particular chapter more expensive than inaction anywhere else in this book. Every other pattern described so far involves an active behavior that can simply be stopped — a payment cancelled, a rule loosened, a comparison named and set down. This chapter's cost isn't produced by doing something. It's produced by not doing something, which means there's no single moment of relief available from simply stopping. The only way through is forward, through action, which is precisely why avoidance feels so tempting and costs so much.

The primary cost of not actively pursuing this kind of reconstruction is a persistent, low self-efficacy that, left unaddressed, tends to become self-fulfilling. A person who avoids financial tasks out of a belief they'll fail at them never accumulates the mastery experiences that would prove otherwise, which means the belief, however inaccurate at its origin, gets reinforced by the very avoidance it produces — a genuinely vicious cycle that requires deliberate interruption, because it will not resolve simply by waiting for confidence to arrive before acting.

There's a cost, closely related, to how long the reconstruction takes overall. Someone who defers financial decisions indefinitely out of a mistaken belief in their own incapacity delays the entire process this book has been describing since Chapter 1 — the actual construction of a new, individually held financial identity — because that identity can only be built through the accumulation of exactly the mastery experiences avoidance prevents. Every month of deferred taxes, deferred applications, deferred decisions is a month the new identity doesn't get built, leaving the person suspended, longer than necessary, in the disorienting in-between state this whole book has been describing.

There's a cost to relationships and future partnerships, worth naming honestly. Someone who never rebuilds an independent sense of financial competence often enters future relationships carrying the same division-of-labor assumptions that calcified in the previous one — quickly ceding financial decision-making to a new partner not because it genuinely suits either person's actual interest or skill, but because the old "I'm not the financial one" identity never got tested and disproven, and simply migrates, unexamined, into the next chapter of the person's life.

There's a cost, specific to the third scenario, to genuinely knowing oneself. A person who never does the work of discovering independently held preferences — risk tolerance, financial values, priorities — separate from a negotiated partnership position, arrives at any future major financial decision without a clear, personally examined foundation to build it on. This isn't merely an inconvenience. It leaves a person vulnerable to simply adopting whatever a future partner's preferences happen to be, repeating the exact fusion this book's earlier chapters have described, rather than entering a future partnership as someone who already knows, independently, what they actually want.

There's a cost specific to the fourth scenario worth marking with real care: shame. A person starting mastery-building from a genuinely foundational level, later in life than most of their peers, often carries a private, corrosive embarrassment about the gap itself — a feeling that the starting point should have been reached decades earlier, which can, left unaddressed, become a bigger obstacle to actual progress than the underlying skill gap ever was. Bandura's research is worth returning to directly here: shame about a low starting point is not itself a mastery experience, and dwelling in it doesn't accelerate the building of genuine self-efficacy. It mostly just makes the first small task harder to attempt.

Finally, there's a cost to the broader project this book has been describing throughout: without deliberately pursued mastery experiences, the "new" financial self doesn't actually get built. What exists instead is an absence — the old joint identity gone, and nothing sufficiently solid yet constructed to replace it — which is precisely the disorienting, ungrounded state so many of the earlier chapters have described people getting stuck in. Reconstruction requires action, not just time. Time alone, without deliberate mastery experiences accumulating within it, doesn't reliably produce the confidence this chapter is describing.

The overrides

Deliberately choose one small, low-stakes financial task to complete entirely alone, on purpose, soon. Don't wait for a task to be forced on you by circumstance. Choose something manageable — negotiating a single bill, comparing insurance quotes, filing a simple form — specifically to generate a mastery experience on your own timeline. The task's actual difficulty matters less than the fact that you chose it, executed it, and completed it independently; per Bandura's research, that combination is what actually builds self-efficacy, regardless of how modest the task looks from the outside.

The Move: test the specific skill deficit you've assumed exists, directly, rather than continuing to assume it. If you've internalized a belief that you're "not the financial one," pick the single task most associated with that belief — doing your own taxes, reading your own investment statements, building your own budget from scratch — and do it once, deliberately, expecting it might be hard. Most people discover, the way the man in this chapter did, that the actual skill gap is considerably smaller than the internalized story about it, because the story was often never really about individual capability to begin with.

Interview yourself about your own preferences, separate from any negotiated compromise, before your next major financial decision. Before investing, before a major purchase, before setting a savings goal, ask directly: setting aside what a partner and I used to agree on together, what do I actually want here, on my own terms? This is genuine, sometimes unfamiliar work, particularly for anyone whose adult financial life has mostly existed inside a negotiated partnership — give it real time rather than expecting an instant answer.

Track your own mastery experiences explicitly, in writing, rather than trusting confidence to accumulate invisibly. Keep a simple, ongoing list of independent financial tasks you've successfully completed since the divorce — the lease, the tax return, the negotiated salary, the built budget. This isn't vanity. Per Bandura's research, self-efficacy is built through the felt, remembered experience of past success, and an explicit record gives you something concrete to return to on the days the old, discredited "I'm not capable of this" story tries to resurface.

Separate the origin of an old financial label from its accuracy today. If a label like "the financial one" or "the spender" or "the cautious one" has followed you out of the marriage, ask directly: was this label actually about my aptitude, or was it about a division of labor that made sense inside a specific partnership at a specific time? Most inherited financial labels turn out to be closer to job assignments than personality traits, and job assignments can be, and should be, reassigned when the circumstances that produced them no longer exist.

Let mastery generalize on purpose — notice and name the spillover. After a successful independent financial task, explicitly notice, out loud if possible, the ways it makes an adjacent task feel more approachable. This isn't just a nice feeling to register. Per the self-efficacy research this chapter draws on, naming the generalization actively reinforces it, helping the confidence spread more deliberately across your financial life rather than staying contained to the single task where it first appeared.

If your starting point is genuinely foundational, start smaller than pride wants you to. If you're building financial competence closer to the fourth scenario's starting line than the others in this chapter, resist the urge to prove yourself with an ambitious first task. Choose something genuinely small — opening an account, reading a single statement line by line — and let the mastery experience be modest on purpose. Bandura's research is clear that early, easily achievable successes build a more durable foundation than an ambitious first attempt that risks failure and reinforces the exact shame you're trying to move past.

Enlist a knowledgeable friend for your first attempt at an unfamiliar task, not to do it for you, but to sit beside you while you do it yourself. There's a meaningful difference between someone completing a task on your behalf and someone simply being present while you complete it independently. The first teaches you nothing about your own capability. The second is still, per Bandura's research, a genuine mastery experience — you did the work — while offering enough support to make a genuinely unfamiliar first attempt feel survivable rather than overwhelming.

Give yourself credit for mastery experiences that happened before the marriage, too, not just after it. If you're building confidence from what feels like a genuinely foundational level, it can help to remember that you likely navigated real independent decisions before the marriage began — a first apartment, a first job, a first budget — even if that version of you feels distant now. Those earlier mastery experiences are still real evidence of your own underlying capability; the marriage didn't erase them, it just interrupted the habit of drawing on them.

The Rule to Remember: the name now standing alone on the lease, the account, the tax return isn't proof that you're facing this without support — it's proof that the support was never actually the thing making you capable, you were, the whole time, and now there's finally a form with your name on it to show for it.

Chapter 8 — The Number You Keep Measuring Against

Three years after her divorce, she'd built, by any external measure, a genuinely solid financial life — steady income, real savings, a retirement account growing at a reasonable pace for her age. And still, at least once a week, she found herself running a specific, unbidden comparison: where would her net worth be right now if the marriage had never ended, if the two incomes and the shared expenses and the joint retirement contributions had simply continued uninterrupted for these same three years. The comparison never produced anything useful. It only ever produced a specific, deflating sense that she was behind — behind a version of her own life that had never actually existed, running against a hypothetical rather than against any real, comparable person or circumstance.

What made the comparison particularly stubborn, once she examined it honestly, was that it wasn't really comparing her present to a plausible alternate present. It was comparing her present to an idealized, frictionless extension of the marriage — one where the divorce simply hadn't happened, but where nothing else about the marriage's actual trajectory would necessarily have gone any differently either. She never factored in that the marriage had, by its final two years, become a source of real financial strain in its own right — an expensive, drawn-out disagreement about a business venture her ex-husband had wanted to pursue against her judgment, months of counseling neither of them had budgeted for, the slow erosion of savings during a period neither of them now looked back on especially fondly. The comparison she kept running wasn't fair to her present. It was comparing her real, actual, independently rebuilt life against a fantasy that airbrushed out everything that had actually made the marriage's final years difficult in the first place.

A different version of the same pattern showed up for a man measuring himself against a very different number: his ex-wife's current financial situation, several years after their split, which had improved substantially after she remarried a man with considerably more resources than either of them had ever had during their own marriage. He found himself, more often than he wanted to admit, tracking the visible signs of her

new life — a larger house, a nicer car, vacations he saw in photos his kids showed him — and running an internal comparison that left him feeling, each time, a specific mixture of inadequacy and quiet resentment, even though his own financial life, judged on its own terms, was genuinely healthy and improving steadily.

A third version surfaces for a woman comparing her post-divorce financial trajectory against her sister's, who had never divorced and whose household, by virtue of two continuous incomes over the same span of years, had naturally accumulated more than the woman's single-income household had managed to in the same period. The comparison wasn't really about her sister at all. It was a socially acceptable, easier-to-voice proxy for the harder, more painful comparison against her own former marriage — a way of measuring the same underlying loss without having to name her ex-husband directly every time the feeling surfaced.

A fourth version of this pattern shows up in a domain increasingly common and worth flagging directly: social media. A man eighteen months divorced found himself, most evenings, scrolling through the curated financial signals of his broader friend group's lives — a new kitchen renovation here, a European vacation there, a friend's small business milestone announced with visible pride — and running an involuntary comparison against his own, considerably more modest post-divorce budget. None of what he was seeing was actually representative of anyone's full financial picture; renovations get photographed, credit card debt doesn't, and the platform itself selects, by design, for the highlight rather than the whole. He knew this, intellectually, and it changed almost nothing about how the scrolling made him feel, because the comparison mechanism responds to what's vividly in front of it, not to what a person rationally knows about the limits of the sample.

What's actually happening

This chapter's pattern picks up directly where the previous one left off, worth saying as a bridge: Chapter 7 was about building genuine, felt evidence of your own capability. This chapter is about what can undo that evidence just as quickly — a comparison mechanism that doesn't care how much real progress you've made, only how that progress measures up against whatever target it's currently been pointed at, fairly or not.

The clearest lens here returns to Leon Festinger's social comparison theory, already introduced in Chapter 6, extended in a slightly different direction: Festinger's research established not just that people compare themselves to others, but that the choice of comparison target powerfully shapes how a person feels about their own situation, largely independent of how objectively well that situation is actually going. A person comparing their financial life against a genuinely relevant, achievable peer will generally arrive at a more accurate, more useful sense of their own progress than a person comparing against an idealized hypothetical or an unrepresentative, unusually fortunate individual case — and the three comparisons in this chapter's opening scenes are, each in a different way, comparisons against exactly the wrong target: an airbrushed fantasy that never existed, a single, unusually favorable outcome that isn't representative of typical post-divorce outcomes, and a proxy comparison substituting for a harder, more direct one the person hasn't been ready to name.

This connects to a further, more specific body of research on counterfactual thinking — the psychological process of imagining alternative versions of events that didn't actually happen — most extensively developed by psychologist Neal Roese and collaborators across decades of study. Roese's research has found that counterfactual comparisons, particularly upward ones imagining a better alternative outcome than what actually occurred, reliably produce worse mood and lower life satisfaction than comparisons grounded in actual, real-world reference points, even when the imagined alternative is, on close examination, considerably less certain or less realistic than it feels in the moment of comparing. The woman's "where would I be if the marriage hadn't ended" comparison is a textbook upward counterfactual: it imagines a version of events that removes the divorce while leaving every other variable conveniently unchanged, producing an alternate life that looks strictly better than the real one by construction, because the comparison was built, however unconsciously, to produce exactly that result.

Roese's research also identifies an important asymmetry: counterfactual thinking, while capable of producing real distress when it fixates on unfavorable comparisons, can also serve a genuinely useful function when it's directed toward actionable insight rather than simple rumination — imagining what might have gone differently can, in the right circumstances, generate real, useful lessons for future decisions. The distinction that matters is whether the counterfactual comparison is actually informing a future action, or whether it's simply being replayed, repeatedly, with no productive output — which places this pattern in close relationship to the rumination mechanism described in Chapter 6, now aimed specifically at a hypothetical rather than at a real, settled agreement.

The man's comparison against his remarried ex-wife's new financial situation illustrates a related but distinct mechanism: comparison against an unrepresentative reference case. Research on social comparison has long distinguished between comparisons against a genuinely typical, achievable peer and comparisons against an outlier case that happens to be unusually visible — and an ex-spouse who remarries into significantly

more resources is, statistically, closer to an outlier than a representative benchmark for what post-divorce financial recovery typically looks like. Measuring your own, entirely typical financial recovery against someone else's unusually fortunate outcome will reliably produce a distorted, unnecessarily discouraging sense of your own progress, not because your progress is actually inadequate, but because the yardstick itself was never a fair one to begin with.

The sister comparison, finally, illustrates a phenomenon worth calling by its name: displacement, a well-documented pattern in emotional processing where a difficult, hard-to-approach feeling gets redirected toward an easier, more socially sanctioned target. Comparing yourself to a sibling's household income is a comparison most people feel comfortable voicing out loud, even to a therapist or a close friend, in a way that "I keep comparing myself to the marriage I would have had" often isn't, because the latter feels, to many people, uncomfortably close to admitting they still wish the marriage had continued. The sister comparison lets the underlying feeling get some air and some processing without requiring the harder,

more vulnerable admission underneath it — useful in the short term, but ultimately a detour around the actual comparison that needs to be examined directly if it's ever going to lose its grip.

The social-media scenario adds a specific, well-documented modern layer to Festinger's original theory: research on social comparison in digital environments has consistently found that curated online content produces an especially distorted comparison sample, because it systematically overrepresents positive financial signals — purchases, renovations, vacations — while almost entirely omitting the debt, stress, and financial strain that so often accompanies them. This isn't a new psychological mechanism so much as an old one operating on a distorted, unusually one-sided diet of comparison data, available at a volume and frequency no earlier generation navigating a divorce ever had to contend with. A person recovering from a divorce is, by the nature of the process, unusually vulnerable to exactly this kind of comparison, at exactly the moment a curated, highlight-reel version of everyone else's financial life is only a few scrolls away.

What it costs you

It's worth pointing out, before the specific costs below, the particular cruelty of this pattern relative to the others in this book: unlike a fortress rule or an unresolved fairness ledger, this comparison actively punishes genuine progress rather than simply failing to acknowledge it. The better a person's real financial life gets, the more material the comparison has to work with, and the more opportunities it finds to manufacture a fresh sense of falling short — which means, perversely, that real success in reconstruction can sometimes make this particular pattern louder rather than quieter, at least until it's named and interrupted directly.

The most direct cost is the one Roese's research would predict: measurable, recurring distress attached to a genuinely solid, improving financial life, simply because the life is being measured against the wrong yardstick. The woman in the opening scene has real, legitimate reasons to feel good about her financial trajectory. The comparison she keeps running prevents her from actually feeling that, replacing earned satisfaction with a manufactured sense of falling behind a version of events that was never guaranteed, and that, on closer honest examination, likely wasn't even as rosy as the comparison assumes.

There's a cost to decision-making itself, worth pausing on directly. A person chronically comparing their financial life against an unfavorable or unrepresentative benchmark often makes worse decisions as a result — taking on more financial risk than their actual situation warrants in an attempt to "catch up" to a fantasy, or conversely, becoming so discouraged by the comparison that they stop engaging with their own financial planning altogether, concluding, inaccurately, that the gap is too large to meaningfully close.

There's a relationship cost, specific to the second scenario, worth spelling out honestly. A man tracking his ex-wife's new, more prosperous life, even privately, risks that comparison eventually surfacing in front of his children — a resentment that, however carefully managed most of the time, has a way of leaking into offhand comments, a tone of voice, a visible reaction to a photo, in ways that can genuinely complicate a child's experience of moving between two households with different financial circumstances, adding an emotional burden onto kids who didn't choose either household's income level and shouldn't be made to feel responsible for the gap between them.

There's a cost to self-worth, particularly relevant here because financial comparison, unlike some other domains, is unusually visible and unusually loaded with cultural meaning about personal success and competence. A person who chronically measures their post-divorce financial recovery against an unrealistic or unrepresentative benchmark risks internalizing a broader, inaccurate story about their own capability and worth — not just "my finances are behind," but "I am behind," a much larger and more corrosive conclusion than the narrow financial comparison actually supports.

Finally, there's a cost to the reconstruction project this entire book has been describing. Genuine reconstruction requires being able to accurately assess your own progress on its own terms, in order to know what's actually working and what genuinely needs attention. A comparison-driven distortion of that assessment — measuring against a fantasy, an outlier, or a displaced proxy — makes it considerably harder to see your own real financial life clearly enough to keep building it well, because the distorted comparison is constantly supplying inaccurate information about how the construction is actually going.

There's a final cost specific to the social-media scenario worth calling out plainly: frequency. A counterfactual fantasy about the marriage, or a comparison against a sister's household, tends to surface periodically, prompted by a specific event. A social media feed supplies fresh comparison material on demand, dozens of times a day if a person lets it, which means this particular version of the pattern has the potential to run far more often, and with far less friction, than any of the other three versions described in this chapter — a genuinely higher-volume cost, worth taking seriously precisely because of how ordinary and unremarkable each individual instance of it feels.

What unites all four versions of this pattern, worth sitting with before the overrides below, is that none of them are actually about the target being compared against. The fantasy, the remarried ex-spouse, the sister, the curated feed — each is simply the current vessel for a comparison instinct that would find a new target the moment the old one lost its power, unless the underlying mechanism itself gets examined rather than merely redirected. Removing one comparison target without addressing the mechanism tends to produce a brief reprieve, followed by a new target arriving to take its place.

The overrides

Identify your comparison target explicitly, and ask whether it's actually representative. The next time you notice yourself in a financial comparison that leaves you feeling behind, name the specific target directly: is this a realistic, achievable peer, or is it a fantasy, an outlier, or a proxy standing in for something harder to name? Simply identifying which category the comparison falls into often drains a significant portion of its emotional force, because the comparison's unfairness becomes visible the moment it's actually examined rather than simply felt.

The Move: replace the counterfactual comparison with your own actual trajectory over time. Instead of measuring your current financial position against a hypothetical version of the marriage that never had to weather any of the marriage's own real difficulties, measure your current position against your own position one year ago, and one year before that. This comparison is not just kinder — per Roese's research on counterfactual thinking, it's also considerably more accurate, because it's grounded in real, known data rather than an imagined alternate history built to look better than reality by construction.

Fill in the missing variables of any counterfactual comparison, deliberately, before trusting its conclusion. If you catch yourself imagining a better alternate life the divorce prevented, force yourself to add back in everything the fantasy conveniently leaves out — the real strain the marriage was actually under, the problems that were never going to resolve themselves, the version of the future that was genuinely, realistically likely rather than the version that simply removes the one variable you wish had gone differently. Most upward counterfactuals collapse considerably once their missing variables get restored.

When comparing against an ex-partner's new circumstances, ask what's actually representative rather

than what's simply visible. A remarried ex-spouse's improved financial situation is one data point, not a benchmark for what your own recovery should look like. Seek out, if it's useful, a broader, more accurate sense of what typical post-divorce financial recovery actually involves — through a financial planner, a support group, or simply a wider set of real comparison points — rather than anchoring your entire sense of progress to the one case you happen to have the most visibility into.

Name the displaced comparison directly, if you suspect one is in play. If a comparison against a sibling, a friend, or anyone else in a comparable life stage keeps producing distress that seems larger than the comparison itself would warrant, ask directly: is this actually about them, or is this an easier way of feeling something harder to name about my own marriage and how it ended? Naming the real comparison, even privately, tends to be more resolving, in the long run, than continuing to process it through an easier substitute that was never actually the source of the feeling.

Build a written record of your own real financial progress, and consult it before any comparison-driven spiral. Similar to the mastery-experience tracking described in Chapter 7, keep a simple, factual record of your own financial milestones since the divorce — debts paid down, savings built, income grown. When a comparison starts to spiral, read the record before doing anything else. It won't erase the comparison instinct entirely, but it gives you a genuine, evidence-based counterweight to reach for instead of the manufactured, unfavorable one the comparison is offering.

Treat a curated feed as a known-biased sample, and limit exposure during active reconstruction. If you notice financial comparison spiraling most often during a specific, identifiable habit — an evening scroll, a particular platform — treat that habit the way you'd treat any other known trigger, and consider a deliberate, temporary limit on it while the rest of this book's reconstruction work is still underway. This isn't a permanent verdict on social media. It's a recognition that a known-biased comparison sample, consulted dozens of times a day, is an unusually heavy weight to carry during an already vulnerable stretch.

Practice naming genuine progress out loud, on a regular schedule, independent of any comparison at all. Once a week or once a month, state plainly, to yourself or to someone else, one concrete way your financial life has improved on its own terms, with no reference point outside your own past. This isn't positive thinking for its own sake. It's a deliberate counterweight to a comparison mechanism that, left alone, will keep supplying an unfavorable yardstick indefinitely, and it gives your own real trajectory equal airtime against the fantasy that keeps trying to outshout it.

When a new comparison target appears, ask what it's replacing. If you notice a fresh comparison surfacing shortly after an old one lost its grip, treat that as useful information rather than a fresh crisis. The mechanism itself, not any single target, is what needs addressing — and recognizing a new target as simply the latest costume the same instinct is wearing tends to drain it of urgency far faster than engaging with it as a brand-new problem each time.

Ask what a fair, representative comparison would actually look like, and seek it out deliberately. Rather than simply avoiding comparison altogether, which is rarely sustainable long-term, look for genuinely representative data — a support group of people navigating similar circumstances, a financial planner who works regularly with divorced clients, published research on typical post-divorce financial trajectories. A fair comparison, deliberately sought, tends to crowd out the unfair one far more effectively than willpower alone.

The Rule to Remember: the number you keep measuring against was never a real place your life could have actually landed — it's a fantasy built to always come out ahead, and no amount of catching up to it will ever feel like enough, because it was never designed to be caught.

Chapter 9 — The Merge You're Afraid to Try Again

Four years after her divorce, she was, by every reasonable measure, in a healthy, promising new relationship — two years in, genuinely compatible, both of them talking, in the comfortable, unhurried way serious couples eventually do, about a future that included moving in together. And every time the conversation turned toward the practical financial questions that moving in together would eventually require — a shared lease, a joint account for household expenses, even something as modest as splitting a grocery bill on a shared card — she felt a specific, physical resistance rise up in her that had nothing to do with her actual feelings about her new partner. She trusted him. She wanted the relationship to work. And still, some part of her treated every proposed financial merger, however small and however reasonable, as a live threat requiring careful, exhausting scrutiny before she could agree to it, if she agreed to it at all.

What eventually helped her name the pattern clearly was a conversation with her partner himself, who, after months of watching her deflect even modest financial integration, asked her gently what she was actually afraid would happen. Her honest answer, when she finally found it, surprised her: she wasn't afraid he'd do what her ex-husband had done. She genuinely didn't believe that. What she was afraid of was simpler and, in its own way, harder to argue with: that merging again, at all, in any form, meant opening herself back up to the specific vulnerability of losing an entire financial identity a second time, regardless of how trustworthy this particular partner turned out to be. The fear wasn't really about him. It was about the mechanism itself — about what merging, as an act, had already cost her once, and what it might cost again if this relationship, too, someday ended.

A different version of the same avoidance showed up for a man three years into a new relationship, who'd become, without quite meaning to, the kind of partner who insisted on splitting every single expense with mathematical precision — down to the dollar, every time, no exceptions, no generosity, no flexibility, regardless of how large or small the expense or how clearly one of them was better positioned to cover it in a given month. His new partner, increasingly frustrated, eventually pointed out that his rigid, ledger-style precision felt less like fairness and more like distance — a way of making sure nothing between them ever became entangled enough to genuinely hurt if it ended, at the cost of the ordinary generosity and flexibility that actually builds trust between two people building a life together.

A third version, closing this book's brief, recurring acknowledgment of the mechanism's reach beyond divorce specifically, surfaces for a widower five years into a new relationship, still maintaining an almost total financial separation from his partner despite a genuinely loving, committed relationship, not out of any specific fear of loss through betrayal, but out of a quieter, harder-to-name reluctance to build a new "ours" that might someday require him to survive dismantling it again, the way he'd once had to dismantle one built over three decades with his late wife.

A fourth version of this pattern, offering a genuinely hopeful counterpoint to the first three, comes from a woman six years past her divorce, in a new marriage now three years old, who described to a friend exactly how she'd worked through this same reluctance rather than simply outgrowing it with time. Early in the new relationship, she'd insisted on total financial separation, almost identically to the woman in this chapter's opening scene. What changed wasn't a single conversation or a sudden loss of fear. It was eighteen months of small, deliberate steps — a shared account for one modest recurring expense first, then two, then a genuine joint conversation about retirement planning that she initiated herself, on her own timeline, once each smaller step had been honored and had produced no repeat of the original harm. By the time she and her new husband merged their finances more fully, the decision didn't feel like a leap of faith. It felt, she said, like something she'd already tested, piece by piece, until there was nothing left to be afraid of that hadn't already been quietly disproven.

What's actually happening

It's fitting that this book's final chapter returns to attachment, the mechanism first introduced in Chapter 2, because everything this book has described — the ledger, the guilt, the fortress, the house, the ghost, the fairness, the name on the new account, the number you keep measuring against — has ultimately been in service of this last question: once a financial self has been rebuilt, individually, deliberately, on its own two feet, is it capable of choosing interdependence again, on purpose, rather than either defaulting into it unconsciously the way the original marriage likely did, or refusing it permanently out of a fear that was never really about the new person in front of you.

The clearest framework for understanding this final pattern comes from attachment theory, introduced in Chapter 2, extended here to its natural conclusion: John Bowlby's foundational research, along with subsequent work by researchers including Mary Ainsworth and, in more recent decades, Sue Johnson's development of emotionally focused therapy grounded directly in attachment research, has documented how a significant attachment rupture — the loss of a major attachment bond, through death, divorce, or the end of a long partnership — can produce a lasting shift toward what attachment researchers describe as avoidant strategies in future relationships: a tendency to limit vulnerability, maintain independence, and resist the kind of deep interdependence that characterized the previous bond, specifically as a protective measure against experiencing that particular kind of loss again. This isn't a permanent, fixed change to a person's attachment style in every case — attachment research has increasingly emphasized that attachment patterns can shift, sometimes considerably, in response to new, corrective relational experiences. But the shift toward caution after a major rupture is real, well-documented, and, importantly, not really a reasoned response to any specific new partner's trustworthiness. It's a generalized protective adaptation, and it will apply itself, indiscriminately, to any new partner, however trustworthy that partner actually is, unless it's deliberately recognized and worked with.

This distinction matters enormously for the three scenes above, because in each case, the resistance to financial merger isn't actually functioning as risk assessment of the current relationship — it's functioning as a categorical avoidance of the entire class of behavior that produced the original loss. The woman in the opening scene explicitly named this once she examined it honestly: her hesitation had nothing to do with genuine doubt about her current partner's character. It was a blanket wariness of merging itself, as an act, regardless of who the merging partner happened to be. That distinction offers real hope alongside the honest diagnosis: a fear that isn't actually about the current relationship is, in principle, more addressable than a fear grounded in real, present-tense evidence of risk, because it responds to deliberate, gradual, corrective experience in a way that a genuinely well-founded suspicion wouldn't.

There's a second piece here, drawn from research on trust repair and interpersonal risk, a body of work within relationship science examining how people rebuild the capacity for vulnerability after it's been significantly damaged. This research has consistently found that trust and vulnerability rebuild most reliably through small, graduated exposures — modest acts of trust extended and honored, repeated over time — rather than through either total avoidance or an abrupt, all-at-once leap back into full vulnerability. The man's rigid, dollar-precise expense-splitting represents one common failure mode of this process: a strategy that avoids the graduated exposure altogether by refusing meaningful vulnerability in the first place, which protects against the specific pain of a future merger's collapse but does so at the direct cost of the closeness graduated trust-building would otherwise allow to develop.

The widower's story clarifies an important final point about this mechanism's reach: the resistance to a new financial merger isn't necessarily about a specific fear of repeated betrayal or repeated divorce at all. Sometimes, as in his case, it's a resistance to the raw structural fact of interdependence itself — an unwillingness to build something that would, if lost again through any cause, require surviving that particular kind of dismantling a second time. That matters because it means the overrides ahead need to address something slightly broader than simply rebuilding trust in a specific new person. They need to address a person's relationship to interdependence as a category, separate from any judgment about whether this particular new partnership actually warrants that interdependence.

One final, hopeful piece, drawn again from Bonanno's resilience research introduced in Chapter 1: most people, across most kinds of significant loss including divorce, demonstrate considerably more capacity for eventual adaptation and renewed close connection than either they themselves or the broader culture around loss typically expects. The caution described throughout this chapter is a real, well-documented, entirely understandable protective response. It is not, for most people, a permanent verdict on their future capacity for trust and genuine partnership — which is worth holding onto directly, as this book's final chapter closes, alongside the honest acknowledgment of how real and how sticky the caution can feel while it's actively running.

Return to the fourth scenario for a genuine demonstration of the graduated trust-building research in practice, rather than only in theory. What made her eighteen-month process work wasn't the passage of time alone — plenty of people spend far longer than eighteen months still fully avoidant, as the other scenarios in this chapter show. It was the deliberate structure of small steps, each one honored, each one producing real, felt evidence that this new relationship wasn't a repeat of the old harm. Time without structured, graduated exposure tends to leave avoidant patterns largely intact. Time with it, as her story illustrates, is what actually lets the nervous system update its own risk assessment, one small proof at a time.

As this book's final mechanism section closes, here's what distinguishes a person who's done the work described across these nine chapters from a person who hasn't, because the difference isn't the absence of fear. Both people feel some version of the hesitation this chapter describes when a new relationship raises the question of merging again. The difference is what happens next: one person recognizes the fear as a known, named mechanism — attachment doing exactly what attachment is built to do after a real rupture — and works with it deliberately, in small steps, toward a genuine choice. The other lets the fear make the decision by default, indefinitely, mistaking a reflex for a verdict. Every chapter in this book has, in its own domain, been describing that same distinction. This final chapter simply asks it one more time, about the biggest and most consequential financial decision a person will ever face twice: whether to build a shared life again.

What it costs you

It's fitting that this final chapter's costs are, in a real sense, the sum of every cost named across the book so far. A person who never revisits their capacity for interdependence hasn't just limited a single future relationship — they've let the original rupture have the final word over the entire, longer arc of their life, which is precisely the outcome every override in every previous chapter has been quietly working against.

The most direct cost is to the new relationship itself, illustrated clearly in the man's story: rigid, categorical avoidance of financial interdependence, applied indiscriminately regardless of a new partner's actual demonstrated trustworthiness, communicates a message the new partner didn't earn and likely doesn't deserve — that they are, functionally, being treated as a repeat of the risk that caused the original harm, however unfair that framing is to someone who had no part in it. Left unaddressed, this can genuinely erode a new relationship's growth, not because anything is actually wrong between the two people, but because one partner's protective strategy is preventing the ordinary depth of trust a healthy long-term partnership generally requires.

There's a cost to the person carrying the caution as well, worth stating honestly. A financial life kept permanently, categorically separate from a genuinely trustworthy partner forfeits real, practical benefits — shared financial planning, combined resources that could accelerate goals neither partner could reach as quickly alone, the genuine efficiency and support a well-functioning financial partnership can provide. This isn't an argument that every relationship should merge finances, or that merging finances is inherently better than maintaining separateness by genuine mutual choice. It's a narrower point: caution driven by unexamined fear rather than by a couple's actual, freely chosen values produces a worse outcome than either full merger or full separation chosen deliberately, because it's not actually a choice at all. It's a reflex wearing the costume of one.

There's a cost to the reconstruction project this entire book has been describing, in its final and perhaps most important form. A person who never revisits their capacity for financial interdependence hasn't actually completed the rebuilding this book set out to describe — they've built a defended, independently competent financial self, which is real and valuable progress, but stopped one step short of a fuller reconstruction: the capacity to choose interdependence again, deliberately, from a position of genuine strength rather than from the old, pre-divorce position of assumed default merger, or from the opposite extreme of permanent, fear-driven separateness.

There's a cost, too, to the specific relationship being built with each individual new partner, worth naming as this book closes: every one of the nine chapters in this book has, in its own way, been about the difference between a reflexive, unexamined response to money and a deliberate, examined one. A financial life kept permanently separate purely out of unexamined fear is, in its own way, just as unexamined as the automatic joint merger many people build without a second thought in a first serious relationship. The goal was never to swing from one unexamined default to its opposite. It was to arrive, eventually, at genuine choice.

Finally, there's a cost worth marking honestly and without false comfort: some caution, after a real and significant loss, is not a pattern to be dismantled entirely, and this book has no interest in arguing that a person should feel obligated to merge finances again on any particular timeline, or at all, if genuine reflection leads them to conclude that separateness suits their actual values and their actual life. The cost described in this section applies specifically to caution that's running on autopilot, unexamined, applied indiscriminately regardless of the actual partner or actual circumstances in front of a person right now. Caution that's been genuinely, deliberately chosen is not a cost. It's simply a decision, made the way every decision in this book has ultimately been arguing you deserve to make them: on purpose, with clear eyes, rather than by reflex.

The overrides

Separate the fear of the mechanism from the fear of the specific person. Ask directly, honestly: am I hesitant because something about this particular partner has given me a genuine reason for caution, or am I hesitant because merging, as an act, cost me something significant once before, regardless of who I'm merging with this time? These call for different responses. A specific, evidence-based concern deserves real attention and possibly real boundaries. A generalized wariness of the mechanism itself deserves gentle, deliberate exposure rather than permanent avoidance.

The Move: choose one small, graduated act of financial trust, and let it be genuinely small. Rather than either avoiding all financial interdependence or attempting a full merger all at once, choose one modest, bounded act of shared financial vulnerability — a shared small expense fund, a single joint bill, a transparent conversation about money without any account actually changing hands yet. Per the research on graduated trust-building, small successful experiences of shared vulnerability, repeated over time, do more to genuinely rebuild capacity for interdependence than either total avoidance or a single large leap that outpaces where you actually are.

Name the fear to your partner directly, the way the woman in this chapter's opening scene eventually did. A partner who understands that your hesitation is about a past mechanism rather than about their own trustworthiness is far better positioned to be patient, supportive, and genuinely helpful in the graduated process ahead than a partner left to guess, and possibly to misread the caution as a judgment about them specifically, which is rarely what it actually is.

Distinguish deliberate separateness from defensive separateness. If, after real reflection, you conclude that maintaining largely separate finances genuinely suits your values, your relationship, and your considered preferences — not just your fear — that's a legitimate, healthy choice this book has no interest in talking you out of. The test isn't whether you merge. It's whether the decision, whichever direction it goes, was actually made on purpose, examined honestly, rather than defaulted into by an old fear that never got a fair hearing.

Revisit the decision periodically, rather than treating an early instinct as permanent. Trust-building and comfort with interdependence tend to shift over the life of a relationship, sometimes considerably. A boundary that made sense in a relationship's second year may no longer reflect where you or your partner actually are by its fifth. Build in an occasional, deliberate check-in — not to pressure movement in either direction, but to make sure the current arrangement still reflects a genuine, current choice rather than an old decision quietly running on inertia.

Hold Bonanno's finding close as you do this work: most people recover more capacity for trust than they expect to. If the caution feels, right now, like a permanent condition rather than a phase, it's worth remembering directly that the research on resilience after significant loss consistently finds the opposite to be true for most people, most of the time. The caution you feel today is not a life sentence. It's a real, current, entirely reasonable protective response, doing exactly what it evolved to do — and, like most protective responses, it tends to soften considerably once it's given real, safe, repeated evidence that this particular new circumstance isn't the old one wearing a different face.

Let each graduated step actually finish before adding the next one. The woman in this chapter's fourth scenario didn't rush her eighteen months, and that pacing was part of what made it work. Resist the urge to move to the next level of financial interdependence simply because a deadline, a milestone, or someone else's timeline suggests you should. Let each small step genuinely settle, and notice, honestly, whether the earlier fear has actually quieted before building on top of it.

Notice the difference between a partner asking for patience and a partner asking you to abandon caution entirely. A healthy new partner, informed honestly about the mechanism behind your hesitation, will generally welcome a graduated pace. A partner who responds to that honesty with pressure to move faster than feels genuinely safe is giving you real, current information worth taking seriously — not proof that your caution was wrong, but a legitimate data point about this specific relationship, separate from the general work of loosening an old, generalized fear.

Celebrate each graduated step as its own real accomplishment, not just as progress toward a larger goal. The woman in this chapter's fourth scenario didn't just tolerate her eighteen months of small steps — each one, taken on its own terms, represented a genuine act of courage worth recognizing in the moment, not only in hindsight. Treating each small act of shared financial vulnerability as a real, complete accomplishment, rather than merely a means to an eventual merger, makes the whole graduated process considerably more sustainable to actually live through.

The Rule to Remember: the reluctance to merge again isn't proof that you haven't healed — it's proof that the last merger meant something real enough to leave a mark, and the work now isn't erasing that mark, it's deciding, on purpose, whether you're ready to risk one like it again.

Before You Go

Before you go, think about the specific moment somewhere in these pages that landed closest to home — the parking lot after the first solo bank account, the automatic transfer you can't quite bring yourself to cancel, the house payment that's become the last thread still holding onto a life that's already over on paper. That moment is real, and it was never an overreaction. It's what it actually looks like when a financial identity built for two people has to become one built for a single person, alone, usually while everything else in life is also asking something of you at the same time.

You've moved through nine shapes of the same underlying rupture across this book, and it's worth flagging plainly what they had in common. The ledger that used to say "ours," dissolving a piece of self along with the account. The guilt that kept paying down a debt that was never really about money. The fortress built from real rubble, defending against threats that had already passed. The house, the business, the object that wouldn't let go because letting go meant admitting a future you'd once pictured wasn't happening anymore. The ghost still consulted at the kitchen table, running a rulebook its author no longer has any right to enforce. The fairness that couldn't stop being litigated at midnight, chasing a verdict the math was never going to provide. The name finally standing alone on the lease, the tax return, the account — proof of a competence that had been there all along, just never tested solo. The number you kept measuring your real, improving life against, a fantasy that was never a fair fight to begin with. And finally, the reluctance to merge again, protecting against a loss that already happened once, in a body that hasn't yet been convinced it's safe to try.

Here is the thesis this whole book has been circling, said as plainly as it can be said: you are not trying to recover the financial self you had during the marriage. That self was never fully yours to begin with — it was a joint structure, co-authored, and it dissolved, correctly and permanently, the moment the partnership that built it ended. What you're actually doing, in every chapter of this book, in every account you've opened alone and every reflex you've caught and examined, is building someone new. Not a repaired version of the old self. A first version of this one.

So here is the one practice worth carrying out of these pages and into the actual, ongoing work ahead: the next time an old reflex fires — the reach for a consultation partner who isn't there, the guilt over a payment you no longer owe, the fortress rule that's protecting you from a threat that's already passed — pause and ask one question before acting on it. *Is this decision actually about what's in front of me right now, or is it about what happened before?* You won't always get a clean answer. But asking the question, consistently, is most of the distance between a financial life still quietly run by a marriage that's over and a financial life that's genuinely, finally your own.

If you take nothing else from these pages, take this: the disorientation you've felt somewhere in this book — in a parking lot, at a dealership, over a spreadsheet at midnight — was never a sign that you were failing at your own recovery. It was the sound of real construction, which is loud, and uneven, and rarely looks like progress while it's actually happening. Every person in this book, real in shape even where the specific details were built for clarity rather than drawn from a single life, was doing the same hard, unglamorous work: building a financial self from a foundation that had, without their consent, been cut in half.

Consider keeping a simple, private note of your own as you keep going — not a formal document, just a record of the specific reflex you recognized most while reading this book, and one small, concrete way you're going to practice responding to it differently. Revisit it in six months. You are very likely to find that the reflex has quieted, not because it was erased in a single insight, but because you kept giving your nervous system new, repeated evidence that the old danger has passed and the new life, run by you alone, is actually safe to build.

It's worth acknowledging honestly, as this book closes, that some of what it's described won't resolve on any tidy timeline, no matter how faithfully you apply what's here. A marriage that ended badly enough, or lasted long enough, leaves marks that a single book, however carefully built, cannot fully smooth over. This book was never going to make the reconstruction painless. What it can do, and what it's tried to do across these nine chapters, is give the reconstruction a shape, a set of names, and a set of concrete moves to try instead of the quiet, unexamined defaults that guilt, fear, and old habit will otherwise happily supply on your behalf.

It's worth saying something directly to whichever version of you picked up this book, because the nine chapters ahead described several quite different starting points, and you may recognize yourself in more than one. If you're the reader still avoiding the portfolio statement, still unable to open it two years on, this book isn't asking you to stop grieving on anyone else's schedule — it's asking you to notice when the avoidance has quietly become the standing strategy rather than a passing wave. If you're the reader who built the fortress, the elaborate, disciplined, admirable-looking system that's slowly closing off a life alongside the danger it was built to keep out, this book isn't asking you to abandon caution — it's asking you to teach that caution to tell the difference between the threat that already happened and the ordinary decisions that only resemble it. If you're the reader still paying an ex-spouse's bill you no longer owe, or still consulting a ghost at the kitchen table, or still measuring your very real progress against a fantasy that was never fair, none of that makes you behind, or broken, or worse at this than anyone else going through it. It makes you exactly as human as everyone else in these pages, working through a rupture almost nobody warned you would be this specific, this disorienting, or this quietly lonely.

There's a broader point worth saying as this book closes, one that connects back to the mitigation this book opened with: everything described across these nine chapters applies, in its own proportion, to anyone whose financial identity was built jointly and then had to become individual again, regardless of which legal instrument, or lack of one, marked the ending. If you came to this book navigating the end of a long partnership rather than a formal divorce, or grieving a spouse rather than divorcing one, the mechanisms in these pages were built with you in mind too, even though divorce remained this book's central, primary subject throughout. The financial self doesn't check paperwork before it decides how hard a separation is going to be. It responds to the depth of what was actually built, and what was actually lost.

There's one final thing worth saying, addressed less to the mechanisms this book has spent nine chapters naming and more to whatever part of you picked this book up in the first place, looking for something. Somewhere between the parking lot and the lease application and the midnight recalculating, most readers of a book like this one are also quietly asking a bigger, less financial question: whether they're going to be okay. This book can't answer that question directly — no book can, and any book that claims to is promising more than it can deliver. What it can offer is a smaller, more honest claim, worth carrying forward past the last page: every pattern named in these chapters is a pattern people move through, not a pattern people stay stuck in forever, and the moving through tends to happen exactly the way it's happened in every scene across this book — unevenly, imperfectly, one deliberately examined decision at a time, until one day the reflexes that used to run the whole show have quietly become the exception rather than the rule.

The financial identity you had inside the marriage is gone. It was never going to come back, no matter how long you waited or how carefully you grieved it. What's ahead instead is something better than a restoration, even if it doesn't feel that way yet: a financial self that belongs entirely to you, built by no one but you, answerable to no one's rulebook but the one you choose, deliberately, on purpose, from here forward.

Notes & Further Reading

The mechanisms described in this book draw on real, established research in psychology, behavioral economics, and relationship science. This book is a work of synthesis and application, not original research — every named finding below belongs to the researchers credited, and readers interested in going deeper should start with their original work.

Chapter 1 — The Ledger That Used to Say "Ours." The self-expansion model, describing how close relationships lead partners to cognitively include each other's traits and resources as part of the self, was developed by psychologists Arthur Aron and Elaine Aron across decades of relationship research, including the widely used Inclusion of Other in the Self scale they developed to measure this overlap directly. Research on grief and adaptation, including the finding that most people demonstrate greater resilience after significant loss than commonly expected, draws on the work of psychologist George Bonanno. Disenfranchised grief — loss that isn't socially recognized or validated through customary mourning rituals — was formally developed as a concept by grief researcher

Kenneth Doka.

Chapter 2 — The Guilt You Keep Paying Down. Loss aversion and the broader research on how losses and gains are weighted asymmetrically draws on the foundational work of psychologists Daniel Kahneman and Amos Tversky, referenced elsewhere in this library. Attachment theory originates with the work of John Bowlby, extended significantly by Mary Ainsworth's research on attachment patterns. The distinction between guilt and shame as distinct moral emotions, including guilt's action-oriented, corrective structure, draws on the research of psychologist June Tangney. Research on anticipatory anxiety and threat overestimation draws on the broader clinical literature on anxiety and worry.

Chapter 3 — The Fortress You Built From the Rubble. Locus of control was developed as a foundational psychological construct by Julian Rotter. Research on psychological flexibility and the costs of rigid, rule-bound behavior draws on the work of psychologist Steven Hayes and collaborators in developing acceptance and commitment therapy. The availability heuristic, describing how vivid, recent, personally significant examples distort probability judgment, was documented by Daniel Kahneman and Amos Tversky as part of their broader research program on judgment under uncertainty.

Chapter 4 — The House That Won't Let Go. Possible selves theory, describing the future-oriented self-representations that motivate present behavior, was developed by psychologists Hazel Markus and Paula Nurius. Research on self-continuity and identity persistence across major life transitions draws on identity development scholarship extending from Erik Erikson's foundational work.

Chapter 5 — The Ghost at the Kitchen Table. Research on habit formation and automaticity, including the finding that established habits persist independent of their original motivating relationship, draws on the extensive work of psychologist Wendy Wood. Cognitive schema research, describing the mental frameworks people use to organize and interpret experience, draws on the broader cognitive psychology literature on schema theory. The transmission of modeled behavior to a new observer draws on Albert Bandura's social learning research, referenced again in Chapter 7.

Chapter 6 — The Fairness You Can't Stop Litigating. Equity theory, examining how people judge fairness through input-to-outcome ratios relative to a comparison other, was developed by psychologist J. Stacy Adams. Social comparison theory traces to Leon Festinger's foundational 1954 research, referenced elsewhere in this library. Research on rumination, and its distinction from productive reflection, draws on the extensive work of psychologist Susan Nolen-Hoeksema.

Chapter 7 — The Name on the New Account. Self-efficacy theory, including the central role of mastery experiences in building durable confidence, was developed by psychologist Albert Bandura across decades of research. Research on preference construction, examining how stated preferences are often actively built rather than simply retrieved, draws on the broader decision-science literature on constructed preferences.

Chapter 8 — The Number You Keep Measuring Against. Social comparison theory, referenced again here, continues to draw on Leon Festinger's foundational work. Research on counterfactual thinking, including the distress associated with upward counterfactual comparisons, draws on the work of psychologist Neal Roese and collaborators. Research on social comparison within digital and social media environments draws on the broader, growing literature applying Festinger's original framework to curated online content.

Chapter 9 — The Merge You're Afraid to Try Again. Attachment theory, referenced again here, draws on the foundational work of John Bowlby and Mary Ainsworth, extended into adult romantic attachment by subsequent researchers including Sue Johnson's development of emotionally focused therapy. Research on trust repair and graduated vulnerability in rebuilding interpersonal trust draws on the broader relationship-science literature on trust and closeness, referenced again from Bonanno's resilience research introduced in Chapter 1.

Any errors of interpretation or application in how these findings are described are the author's alone. This book simplifies genuinely complex research for a general audience; readers who want the full nuance should go to the original sources.

About

The Divorce Instinct comes from the studio behind The Money Instinct project — a psychology-of-money brand built on one premise: the gap between knowing what to do with money and actually doing it is rarely about information. It's about the wiring underneath the decision. This book turns that same lens toward a rupture most money books never address directly at all — not how a couple should divide their finances during a divorce, but what happens, psychologically, to the financial self that has to survive that division and rebuild afterward, alone.

If you're reading this as part of a larger engagement with the rest of this library, you'll notice this book draws on mechanisms introduced elsewhere — loss aversion, social comparison, attachment, self-efficacy — and extends them into a domain the earlier books don't fully cover: the unwinding of an already-merged financial identity back into an individual one, rather than the building or transfer of one. If this is the first book of the library you've picked up, everything here stands on its own; no prior reading is required, and every mechanism is explained fully within these pages.

Every book in this library follows the same underlying commitment: real psychological research, honestly credited, never inflated into something more dramatic than the evidence supports, applied to a specific, common, deeply human pattern that money makes visible. This book is not a substitute for legal, financial, or therapeutic guidance during or after a divorce, and it was never meant to be — those decisions deserve qualified professionals who know your specific circumstances. What this book offers instead is the part no professional typically hands you off the shelf: a clearer understanding of the psychological work underneath the paperwork, so that the financial life you build next is built on purpose, examined and chosen, rather than assembled by default out of guilt, fear, and habit left over from a life that's already ended.

A note on the scenes throughout this book: every person described in these pages is a composite, built for psychological clarity rather than drawn from any single real account. The mechanisms are real, documented, and credited to the researchers who identified them. The people are not. Any resemblance to a specific reader's specific life is a reflection of how common these patterns actually are, not a description of any one person's story.

Before You Close This Book

If even one of these nine patterns felt like it was describing you specifically, there's a next step. A short reflection — identifying which of these patterns is most active in your own financial life right now — helps you see not just which chapter to reread, but which single reflex to start examining first.

The full system, worked examples, and a companion set of reflection guides live at The Money Instinct's home online.

The rupture got you this far, running quietly underneath decisions you've been half-making for months or years. Now you know its shape, where it comes from, and what to build instead of what habit, guilt, or fear would otherwise build for you by default.

Also in the Series

Every book in The Money Instinct library stands on its own — read them in any order. If this one was useful, the library continues:

The Money Instinct

The Secrecy Instinct

The Underearning Instinct

The Shame Instinct

The Panic Instinct

The Merge Instinct

The Ceiling Instinct

The Windfall Instinct

The Control Instinct

The Legacy Instinct

The Comparison Instinct

The Enabling Instinct

The Austerity Instinct

The Paralysis Instinct

The Retirement Instinct

The Enough Instinct

The Overconfidence Instinct

The Vigilance Instinct

The Generosity Instinct

www.ingramcontent.com/pod-product-compliance
Lightning Source LLC
LaVergne TN
LVHW010718061126
851857LV00014B/1236